H7

4—

DREAMS FOR SALE

by the same author

Bound and Gagged
Clown Princes and Court Jesters (with Samuel Gill)
Continued Next Week
World of Laughter
Kops and Custards (with Terry Brewer)
Collecting Classic Films
Winners of the West

DREAMS FOR SALE

*The Rise and Fall
of the
Triangle Film Corporation*

by
KALTON C. LAHUE

South Brunswick and New York: A. S. Barnes and Company
London: Thomas Yoseloff Ltd

© 1971 by A. S. Barnes and Co., Inc.
Library of Congress Catalogue Card Number: 79-124206

A. S. Barnes and Co., Inc.
Cranbury, New Jersey 08512

Thomas Yoseloff Ltd
108 New Bond Street
London W1Y OQX, England

ISBN 0-498-07684-9
Printed in the United States of America

For Julie and Kevin

Contents

	Preface	9
	Acknowledgments	11
1	The Daring Young Man with His Movie Machine	15
2	The Star Boarders	32
3	A One Night Stand	48
4	The Three-Must-Get-Theres	61
5	For Better—but Worse	77
6	Rascals of Wolfish Ways	91
7	The Cure that Failed	102
8	Cursed by their Beauty	116
9	How Heroes Are Made	134
10	Stout Heart but Weak Knees	149
11	The Late Lamented	162
12	A Rose by Any Other Name	174
13	In the Clutches of a Gang	186
14	His Busted Trust	199
	Epilogue	211
	Index	214

Preface

The early days of the motion picture offered unlimited opportunities to those daring enough to seize the initiative. For some, the "flickers" meant near-instant recognition by millions of the public, who were willing to pay money to see these favorites perform. Others, less talented or fortunate, found their places behind the scenes, making stardom possible for the few. But for a select group, the movies meant virtually unlimited wealth, power and prestige. These were the manipulators, the men who created an industry by their financing, production, distribution and even exhibition of the slender strips of celluloid from which tiny figures danced on a beam of light to emerge larger than life on the silver screen.

In the beginning, the role of manipulator could be assumed by almost anyone with access to a few dollars, a camera and some film. But as time went by and the chaos that passed for movie production was gradually refined into a system, the role of manipulator became more expensive and difficult to assume. If they had a common denominator, it was corruption for cash. While not all followed this route, honesty became a rare and often unrewarded trait far outweighed by greed, deception and ambition. Many who fell victim to the latter became among the most powerful men in the industry; others failed to measure up and paid the price accordingly.

Dreams for Sale is the story of one such man, and in a sense it is the story of early Hollywood, where a man could be bankrupt and unknown one day; admired, respected and even feared the next; bankrupt and forgotten the day after. It is the story of a golden cornucopia which spewed forth $300 million in box-office receipts during 1913 and one among many who came forward to claim his share. Harry Aitken differs slightly from the others—he failed while they succeeded, and yet in his failure lies the formula of their success. His dream was ahead of its time and while only he could answer for its failure, the others would correct his mistakes and bring the dream to life a decade later to form empires.

For many years now, film historians have commented on the innovative aspects of the Triangle Film Corporation, briefly noting in passing its failure to survive, and attributing its untimely demise both to its expensive films and the stage actors who had performed in them, neither of which the public appreciated. This insufficiently accounts for the rapid rise and fall of a multimillion dollar corporation; many films of the period were bad and yet somehow they managed to earn a profit in spite of themselves.

Possessing the talents of the three most successful producers in the business at the time, working under the guiding hand of a masterful organizational juggler and promoter, the Triangle Film Corporation had brought Wall Street financing to the motion picture industry; it is not reasonable to assume that bad pictures alone ruined Triangle. Furthermore, the Triangle claims to exorbitant production costs were highly suspect, as were all of the promotional claims to heavy expenditure in the industry—*everyone* had just completed a million dollar film (or so it seemed) which in reality cost only $25,000. Adjusting the Triangle publicity claims to a plausible figure means that either the films were utterly wretched in themselves, with no redeeming value whatsoever at the box-office (an unlikely circumstance in that day and age), or else there had been a gross leakage somewhere else in the system.

While researching another volume since published, I had the opportunity not only to view a respectable number of Triangle Plays (mainly those from the Ince and Sennett studios), but also a fair number of the competition's films from the same time span, 1915-19. As a result, my curiosity became aroused sufficiently to search out exactly what had brought Triangle to the brink of collapse within one year of its founding. One man imbued the Triangle concept with a Cinderella-like quality which tarnished overnight and led to his eventual ruin.

Acknowledgments

The only writer on cinema history who has bothered to consider or suggest any other reasons for Triangle's failure beyond the standard explanation handed down from one author to another is Gertrude Jobe, whose *Motion Picture Empire* was published by Archon in 1966. Her comments were also brief, but tantalizing, and indirectly led to my investigation, the result of which follows, organized for the general reader.

Those who desire specific and detailed information concerning a particular film or films from the many hundreds released under the Triangle banner, are invited to use the Aitken Collection housed with the Wisconsin State Historical Society in Madison. In 1957, Roy Aitken sold a large portion of the records and data relating to the Triangle Film Corporation, the Triangle Distributing Corporation, the New York Motion Picture Company (including Broncho, Domino and Keystone), Reliance, Majestic and Tri-Stone Pictures. These were acquired and preserved for scholarly use. The Collection is incomplete, as Mr. Aitken withheld certain portions for his own use, but resting in the mass of data (202 volumes) which is available are clear indicators that the Triangle films played only a relatively small part in the organization's demise; they did make money, but not in a quantity sufficient to overcome Triangle's inherent weaknesses. My decision to summarize and generalize the production data for use herein is simply to expedite the story and keep it from becoming an unwieldy maze of figures through which the reader would otherwise be forced to wander. The rest of the story is a matter of public record to be found in the archives of the New York Supreme Court.

Materials at the Academy of Motion Picture Arts and Sciences were made available to me and the excellent memory of Keystone general manager George W. Stout was placed at my disposal for many pleasant Saturday afternoons for confirmation and evaluation of data which no outsider could competently and accurately interpret without having an experienced hand on which to rely. For although the Aitken Collection is invaluable, there are pieces missing and important statistical questions thus remain unanswered. I realize that in answering certain fundamental questions, my efforts have in turn created an entirely new set to which I am presently unable to provide the answers and for that, I apologize. My many thanks to the former Triangle employees who graciously consented to be interviewed and the numerous collectors who made their personal archives mine for a day. Stills from the author's collection were supplemented by the National Film Archive, London and Larry Edmunds Bookshop in Hollywood. Frame enlargements from Triangle films were provided by Kent D. Eastin and San Jose State College, San Jose, California.

DREAMS FOR SALE

1
The Daring Young Man with His Movie Machine

LIKE A FIERY SKYROCKET ON A WARM AUTUMN NIGHT, THE Triangle Film Corporation burst across the motion picture screen on September 23, 1915. While its arc was to be great, it would also be brief, but the impact on an industry would not be quickly forgotten. At the time, its immediate result was electrifying to many of those in attendance, even horrifying to some, depending upon which motion picture stock they held. For Joe Engle of Metro and Winfield Sheehan of Fox Films, it was a realization of their worst fears, but to a smiling Harry E. Aitken, this night was to be a magnificent personal triumph, an apparent vindication of his judgment.

For weeks now, rumors had swept the movie industry with a cumulative effect which produced a chill in the business more bitter and cutting than any wind that ever blew down from the frozen Arctic wastelands. In the unbelievably short space of two months, the fast-talking promoter from Wisconsin had put together the ingredients of a combine which he felt would seriously challenge the established giants of the business and on this night had publicly thrown down the gauntlet. The contest was on in earnest and before the evening had raced by, Engle and Sheehan quickly realized that this competition might prove to be formidable. Neither Metro nor Fox was that well established financially in 1915 and a determined challenge for leadership was already underway from Adolph Zukor of Famous Players—another contender for the crown might upset many well-laid plans.

As the house lights of Broadway's Knickerbocker Theatre had

dimmed, the screen blazed forth bearing a new trademark, and lowering his defenses, an ever-smiling Aitken was able to relax somewhat. For well over an hour, he had paced the length of the lobby, personally welcoming each and every guest who had accepted his invitation to attend the premiere. All of Triangle's officers and its New York employees were present, as were the representatives of his financial backers, whose interest was mixed with a good deal of concern. Noted dignitaries in attendance, from Ignace Paderewski and the William Randolph Hearsts to James Montgomery Flagg and Conte Gianni Bettini, lent an aura far beyond that of the usual premiere of the time.

From Triangle's leasing of the Knickerbocker Theatre to its decoration for the occasion, Harry Aitken had spared no effort or expense to make opening night an auspicious affair. Wearing dainty pantalettes, tastefully edged with Triangle lace that showed below the skirt, and a Triangle hat to frame their smile, each of the carefully selected usherettes blended attractively with the general decor, which also made ample use of the Triangle motif—surely a studied calculation on Aitken's part. After all, with the future which Harry had planned for Triangle, such an investment was absolutely necessary. Justification, if such were needed, rested in the fact that Triangle was entering the select world of the $2.00 motion picture seat and the proper impression had to be made if exhibitors were to be successfully seduced from their present connections to sign with Triangle.

Having suitably set the stage, all Aitken could do now was to wait for the audience's response—the rest was really up to the three films he had chosen as Triangle's initial program. Although every indicator told him that the opening would be a grand success, Harry couldn't bring himself to step inside the darkened theatre —too much was whirling through his mind. At this point, he practically knew the pictures by heart, having sat for what seemed to be interminable hours in the little projection room down the hall from Adam Kessel's office in the Longacre Building. While screening completed film after completed film, sometimes alone, sometimes in company with Adam Kessel, Charlie Baumann[1] and others, Harry had compared the strengths and weaknesses of each one, trying to select those which would provide the greatest audience impact. Critics might accuse Harry Aitken of many things,

---

[1] Sometimes spelled Bauman and accepted by its possessor either way, especially if money were involved.

There never has been another western star who created a wave as great as the legendary William S. Hart. Although exploited by Ince while at Triangle, Hart quickly established himself as the *western actor and rivaled Doug Fairbanks for the title of Triangle's top moneymaker. The potential of his films was so great that when W. H. Productions was formed, it was mainly to reissue the old Hart two-reelers of Mutual days. Many exhibitors automatically assumed that W. H. stood for William Hart (which appears to have been Harry Aitken's intention) and booked the old films under their new titles without question.*

The Disciple *(Ince, 1915)* was on the second Triangle program and proved to be Bill Hart's most elaborate film to the time. Brought in for a mere $7253, in contrast to the huge sums Triangle publicity claimed the organization was expending, this story of a frontier minister who nearly lost his soul was well received by fans. Having departed the two-reel short for features, Hart's career suddenly took on a new luster during the Triangle period.

but none could honestly deny that he was a conscientious showman —and also a good one.

In the end, a weary Aitken had stood up from his seat, rubbed bloodshot eyes and mulled everything over in his mind quickly. It had been impossible to make a firm decision that very same night, but after a refreshing sleep, the exhausted president of the yet-untried Triangle Film Corporation had arrived at a final conclusion; he would open with Tom Ince's *The Iron Strain,* Christy Cabanne's *The Lamb* and Mack Sennett's *My Valet.* Although he had liked almost every film shown him, Aitken felt that he had been forced to exercise what he considered to be ruthless judgment in selecting those three he felt to be the very strongest of the offerings.

Pacing back and forth now in the Knickerbocker's lobby, Harry was still certain that he had made the right decision, but acknowledged to himself that an outside possibility of error always existed. That humble touch of modesty was seldom apparent even to his closest friends, but it was there just the same; Harry was afraid that if shown in public, it would be misinterpreted as a sign of weakness or indecision in a business more akin to a jungle than the civilized world. Shrugging his shoulders, Triangle's chief executive concluded that there was nothing left to do except pray. And pray he did as he stepped into the darkness behind the lobby doors, taking the seat which had been reserved for him. It had been a long, hard crawl into the rarified atmosphere which Triangle was about to enter and Harry had doubted only momentarily that he was the one person capable of meeting the many challenges which the future success of Triangle posed.

After all, he *had* come a long way from Wisconsin in the decade since he and his brother Roy had fought their way into the motion picture business with a series of midwestern film exchanges. Although none of the challenges he had faced in the past equalled that of successfully launching a multimillion dollar corporation, Harry had overcome each one with aplomb and a shrewd mind. Without that kind of track record, he mused, neither of the Aitken boys would be sitting in the Knickerbocker that night.

And a rather formidable track record it was. Harry had every reason to be satisfied with himself. Sitting back in the plush seat, he closed his tired eyes, reflecting on the many twists and turns which the road to success had contained. While the exchange business had proven lucrative enough to open an overseas branch in London, Harry Aitken, who combined the qualities of a daydreamer with those of a stubborn realist in a paradoxical mixture, had looked ahead to production as the source of the golden fleece. Accordingly, he set out to organize the Majestic Film Company in 1911 and for his stars, hired Mary Pickford and her husband Owen Moore from Carl Laemmle's Imp while Uncle Carl was vacationing in Europe. Accomplished on a financial shoestring, Majestic would give the Aitkens at least a toehold in the production arena, but not without its own peculiar brand of nightmares.

Majestic was almost totally dependent from its establishment upon the earned revenue of its films to finance further production and although those early pictures had left a great deal to be desired in most cases, "Little Mary" had scored a resounding hit with exhibitors and fans alike. A booming market which seemingly

Bill Hart's westerns have been highly praised for their realism and Hart tried to be authentic in everything he did on-screen. Here he rolls a cigarette with his left hand in The Square Deal Man *(Ince, 1917), one of his last Triangle pictures.*

could not be satisfied worked in favor of such undercapitalized ventures in those early days of movie making and Majestic bridged that initial period to a point of self-sustenance, but not without a good deal of financial juggling on Aitken's part.

When Laemmle returned from Europe to learn that his prize starlet had been stolen after he had worked so hard to entice her from D. W. Griffith and Biograph, the little German was furious beyond speech. Aitken's audacity was to be repaid shortly when Laemmle's Motion Picture Distributing and Sales Company doubled the percentage which Majestic paid for national distribution of its product. Charging Laemmle with restraint of trade, Aitken immediately filed a complaint against the Sales Company and formed his own distribution outlet, the Film Supply Company of

America, taking the product of ten other companies with him upon a hasty departure from Laemmle's organization.

Meanwhile, another disturbed little man sat in a Chicago hotel room musing over Laemmle's high-handed tactics and wondered if the time was ripe to teach him a lesson. John R. Freuler, president of the small but rapidly growing American Film Manufacturing Company, stared first at a list of names in his hand and then at the snowy Chicago streets outside the La Salle. Almost convinced that he could successfully compete with Laemmle, Freuler decided that with the organizational talents of his one-time partner from the days of the Western Film Exchange of Milwaukee, the coup could be worked.

It's not clear to this day who initially brought Crawford Livingston of the Wall Street firm of Kuhn, Loeb and Company into the picture, but it is reasonable to assume that his presence was the

William S. Hart and Alfred Hollingsworth in Hell's Hinges *(Ince, 1916). As villain Silk Miller, Hollingsworth hired Blaze Tracy (Hart) to run a newly arrived minister out of town.* Hell's Hinges *remains one of Hart's best westerns and film historians regard it today as a classic of the genre.*

direct contribution of the imaginative Aitken. At any rate, Wall Street money flowed in to bankroll Harry's next venture and the Mutual Film Corporation was announced to the trade in March of 1912 with the express policy of buying for distribution through its exchanges any pictures which were available, regardless of the seller's other affiliations. This direct slap at Laemmle was quickly countered by his formation of Universal in June 1912.

But within a few short weeks, Universal was in deep trouble when two ex-bookies stalked out of its second board meeting, taking a key block of film production with them. To add insult to injury, Adam Kessel and Charles Baumann moved their allegiance almost immediately to the new Mutual. Mainly on the strength of Thomas H. Ince's work, the pictures of their New York Motion Picture Company had gained a solid reputation and following with audiences; their six reels weekly promised to give the Mutual a large boost, both in quantity and quality of product.

In aligning themselves with the Mutual, Kessel and Baumann had sold their four Empire exchanges to the new distributing organization, also disposing of their stock in the Carlton Motion Picture Laboratories to Harry Aitken, who now became the guiding genius behind Reliance pictures. As with the majority of such arrangements in the movie business, relations between Aitken and the New York Motion Picture Company executives started off on a high note, only to sour gradually. But that would be in the future and Aitken was faced with other pressing and more immediate problems.

Almost from the very beginning, Harry had clashed head-on with his old acquaintance and partner, John R. Freuler. As Mutual's chief executive, Aitken was to come under a cloud of suspected favoritism and discrimination soon after his tenure began. Freuler and Samuel S. Hutchison, both of the American Film Manufacturing Company, became very unhappy about the manner in which Mutual handled their product, but they were firmly bound by contract to supply Mutual with a specified quantity of films for distribution and were thus unable to do much more than grumble loudly in an effort to make life as miserable as possible for Aitken.

In the end, it had remained for Charles J. Hite of Thanhouser to act as the binder of wounds, keeping peace within the family. But Hite's tragic death in 1914 removed him from the scene and shortly even the occasional meetings between Aitken and Freuler became acrimonious shouting matches. Business arrangements were worked out on a lower executive level, as the top corporate posts were stalemated in every direction. Freuler and Hutchison's discontent was further aggravated by the treatment which Mutual began to accord their "Masterpieces." The original agreement had specified that the distributor would handle a special series of feature pictures to be known as "Mutual Masterpieces," features whose quality supposedly rose far beyond that of the routine films released by Mutual and so commanded a premium rental fee from exhibitors. With Mutual's five major producers participating in the "Masterpiece" series, release revolved in a circle so that each firm should have been represented by a new feature every five weeks.

Unfortunately, Aitken began rejecting more and more of the features not produced by his own companies (Reliance and Majestic) as unworthy of "Masterpiece" status. Having wooed D. W. Griffith away from the Biograph in October 1913, Aitken possessed perhaps the most creative director in the business at that time and whose only real competition came from the New York Motion Picture Company's Tom Ince. Many in the industry regarded Griffith as the "Master" director and Freuler and Hutchison soon began referring contemptuously to the "Masterpiece" series as "Griffith-pieces," an open claim that their features were being deliberately ignored in favor of those produced by Griffith. As producers, this state of affairs hurt their reputations, egos and pocketbooks and Aitken's steadfast refusal to reconsider his position in the matter was not to be forgotten.

Harry had further alienated the Mutual directors by organizing the Continental Features Corporation to sell certain of his big pictures independently and outside the auspices of the Mutual, notably those from the production bin of Ince. While these moves set the stage for an eruption of passion on the part of his adversaries, Aitken's personality compounded his troubles and tended to cloud the issues. Although a hard-driving individual, Harry was often obstinate and single-minded in reaching a conclusion. Confident to a point beyond question in his own abilities to command the situation, he longed for the respectability which was associated in the industry with power and enjoyed bringing his talents for persuasion and organization to bear; Harry Aitken was seldom happier than during those moments when he was engaged in the wheeling and dealing of high finance.

As a result, Harry could be looked upon as a professional gambler at this point, something of a semi-legitimate confidence man who could take a risky venture, paint it as a reasonably sound investment and convince those present of its strengths as he went along. Once things got underway, Aitken would then try to cover every possible avenue of failure and often wound up doing a spectacular juggling act. In all fairness, it must be pointed out that as an entrepreneur and producer, he possessed more imagination than many of his contemporaries and was firmly committed to what he felt was the best that money could buy. Triangle, his most imaginative and spectacular venture, was still more than a year in the future, but by early 1914 Harry's fertile mind had nurtured the germ of an idea, one which surfaced periodically as he tried to fend off Freuler and jockey for a more favorable position with Mutual's other board members.

This frame enlargement from Hell's Hinges *(Ince, 1916) is a typical example of the elaborate subtitles which decorated Hart's Triangle westerns, in contrast to the barren backgrounds used with other Triangle Plays.*

Unfortunately, this was not to be. After having committed Mutual to a $40,000 share in Griffith's production of *The Clansman* (released as *The Birth of a Nation*), the enthusiastic speculator and promoter was forced to back down and pick up the tab himself, taking a loan on his Majestic stock to help raise sufficient money to cover the transaction. While this soon proved to be a most fortunate circumstance for him, as the investment was returned many times over, it also served notice to those interested that the reign of Harry Aitken as Mutual's chief executive was in serious jeopardy. Thus the germ became a seedling which began to grow faster and faster, reaching full bloom in May 1915, when Mutual's board of directors met.

By that time, there was much animosity within the corporate offices and most of it was focused on the president. While Aitken was dividing his time among his many interests, Freuler had feverishly contacted the 700 stockholders to line up sufficient support in his bid to unseat the incumbent president, and as a result the election of the chief officer for the coming year proved to be a cut-and-dried affair, with Freuler winning easily. The bell had tolled for Harry Aitken and he knew it. Offering to sell his large block of Mutual stock to the new president, Harry marched out of the office, picked up his hat and went for a long walk. Unknowingly, Freuler confidently settled his bulk behind the helm of a slowly sinking ship and smilingly predicted a rosy future now that Aitken was out.[2]

Aitken had discussed his idea in general with Kessel and Baumann, whose tendency to side with the ex-president in his moments of tribulation now made them keen candidates for discrimination at Freuler's hands. But Kessel and Baumann had their own particular quarrel with Mutual, for the Freuler bloc had refused to allow a renegotiation of their Keystone contract and the two ex-bookies were hardly able to get a decent night's sleep knowing that Mutual was making more money on their Sennett comedies than they were. It was a replay of 1912 and the New York Motion Picture Company was only too eager to escape the Mutual clutches for friendlier hands. Aitken's new plan was the best thing Kessel and Baumann had been offered in years and they readily agreed to

[2] Freuler's one fortunate stroke was in luring Charlie Chaplin away from Essanay in 1916 for the sum of $670,000. After Chaplin's series of 12 comedies were completed, he went over to First National and Mutual struggled on into 1919 before collapsing completely. Its history without Aitken bears a peculiar external resemblance to the checkered career of Triangle with Aitken.

Winifred Westover, who married and divorced William S. Hart in the twenties, had an appeal all her own yet failed to achieve any measure of screen fame.

join him once arrangements had been made for capitalization and their Mutual contract had been completed.

Almost as if he were being pushed by an invisible hand, Harry's stroll took him to New York's financial district. It was money he needed to checkmate Freuler and Mutual, money in almost unheard of quantities; enough to coax the best talent in the business

When Bill Hart left Triangle, the company was left without a western star. H. O. Davis took Roy Stewart out of evening clothes and put him in the saddle. Among the best films Triangle produced during 1918, Roy's westerns were tough-as-leather imitations of the Hart style directed by Cliff Smith, who emerged as a leading director of horse operas during the twenties. Stewart created quite a following, spending much of the next decade in western garb.

into his corner. While Felix Kahn and Crawford Livingston had been of great help in the past, it would be useless to approach them this time; dangerous even, for both men were members of the Majestic, Reliance and Mutual boards of directors. This had resulted from Harry's earlier efforts at financing which had been so successful that he had even persuaded both men to buy stock personally in the companies. To approach them now with the proposition he had in mind would be sheer folly.

This fact had been driven home hard when Aitken had attempted to justify his investment of Mutual funds in Griffith's costly production of Thomas Dixon's novel, *The Clansman*. Expecting that his financial backers would respect his judgment and quickly line up on his side, as they had done so often in the past, Harry had been shocked to find that this time he stood alone and that no amount of his talented power of persuasion could change their minds. Although Kahn and Livingston had originally been wary of investing capital in the fly-by-night motion picture business, Aitken had persuaded them to take a small plunge in 1909, and once in, both found it to their liking. But these men, enamoured as they were of the glamor and girls, the fast living and parties which had started to symbolize the movie world, were also traditionally conservative in their financial thinking and while Harry Aitken's smoothly explained plans made sense as he presented them, both Kahn and Livingston often felt that Harry was inclined to take too much for granted, basing his presentation on too many risky suppositions.

Take Griffith's first super-spectacle as an example. Here was Harry beating the drums for a twelve-reel historical picture at a time when all sound minds agreed that patrons would refuse to watch the screen for three continuous hours. Of course, they overlooked the fact that only a few years before, the same sound minds had rejected the five-reel feature on an identical basis. But production costs on the epic film had run almost out of sight and there was Harry frantically assuring everyone in sight that the man in the street would pay $2.00 for a seat at a time when very few movie houses could get away with charging a quarter admission. While objection after objection had followed, some solid but most without real substance, a convincing picture emerged for the two financial backers—their friend and benefactor had finally succumbed to delusions of his own grandeur. No, Harry Aitken would not be able to turn to Felix Kahn and Crawford Livingston for help this time. He would have to find the necessary money all by himself.

But Wall Street was filled with financial institutions and Harry did not doubt for a single moment that he could ferret out sufficient interest in his new scheme to put together a sound combination of monied interests willing to back the new venture. The greatest challenge of his business career up to that time, the arrangement of this proposition eventually called for Aitken to draw upon every ounce of persuasive talent and showmanship he could muster. Who in his right mind would not show him the door as soon as he pronounced himself to be a motion picture magnate in the market for a $5 million loan?

Interestingly enough, Harry's walk eventually did produce dividends, for the imaginative little entrepreneur had taken great pains to build a sound portfolio in support of his idea. He had also carefully felt the pulse of the financial world several times over the past few months, sounding out his prospects carefully and narrowing them to a select few. The most receptive ear was located at F. S. Smithers and Company, a Wall Street investment banking firm. But convincing Smithers and Company that his idea was viable proved to be a supreme test of Harry's endurance and several fascinating circumstances would come to pass before they agreed to back Aitken and his proposed Sennett-Ince-Griffith Pictures, including a survey of his current financial condition.

By this time, Harry's financial affairs were sufficiently complicated to baffle a team of certified public accountants. He owned many pieces of various organizations on paper, but then again, he really didn't—one had been mortgaged to buy another which in turn was used as collateral for a third and so on. Harry had learned to live with syndicate financing a long time before and this technique, a last resort with many, became a way of life for the promoter. In order to raise enough money to see a film through from script to can, Aitken had often been forced to sell a percentage of the picture's potential earning power to private individuals in return for their making available the necessary capital for production. The gamble was a double-edged one in that either Aitken or his investors stood to take a loss, but after a few tries, Harry's sharp pencil had zeroed in pretty well and he was able to predict results with sufficient accuracy to assure that everyone involved stayed happy.

The great difficulty with this system was that solvency became a much longer road to travel and with Harry's propensity for continually involving himself in new projects, his limited finances remained in a rather strained condition, considerably overextended from a sound fiscal viewpoint. As a result of being forced to syndicate-finance many pictures, Harry had done much of the work and others had benefited with little or no effort on their part. But without their money, the Aitken enterprises would have quite likely withered on the vine. Other early producers had faced the same trap, but few could juggle books with the unerring accuracy of Harry Aitken.

Before he could snare the prospective financial backing, Harry found Smithers and Company insisting that he submit his affairs for restructuring to determine the amount of equity he really possessed.[3] And herein lay the genesis of another nightmare which would return to plague Harry Aitken for many sleepless nights in the near future. While he managed to successfully overinflate the paper value of his Majestic assets to a point well beyond any reasonable resemblance of their actual worth, a section of Santa Monica mountain property which Tom Ince used to film westerns was understood to be owned by his partners-to-be, Kessel and Baumann, and registered as an asset of the New York Motion Picture Company, misrepresenting its worth out of proportion when in reality the property was only leased.

While Aitken's financial condition was really a marginal one in that the façade of his success was draped over a rather low net worth, Harry had shown a profit in whatever he had undertaken in the past decade. But it is quite probable that Smithers and Company, who would have carefully weighed the prospects of the proposed Triangle Film Corporation, gave a heavy emphasis to the smashing financial success of *The Birth of a Nation,* a project in which Harry had invested both time and money as well as faith when the industry scoffed at his chances. As a result of this tremendous success, Harry was basking in the reflected glory of his director; he had made his detractors eat their words and now promised to bring Griffith into the new arrangement—the financiers did not fail to consider the value of this foresighted producer and his director to the scheme.

Having satisfied the preliminary requirements laid down by Smithers and Company, Harry was now able to climb aboard a train heading West, destination unknown to all but his closest business associates. He surfaced a few days later at the Harvey House in La Junta, Colorado, a sleepy little town on the Arkansas River, to await the arrival of D. W. Griffith, Thomas H. Ince and Mack

---

[3] When contacted about this matter, Smithers and Company indicated that their records of this era are no longer in existence and as a result, they could furnish no information or insights on this transaction.

Douglas Fairbanks's arrival was greeted by Sennett's Keystone Cops' Band, a group of minor comics who spent most of their time performing at such functions instead of on the screen. It all made for good clean fun in an era long gone.

Sennett. That Griffith would readily agree to his proposal, Aitken had no doubts. Under contract to Majestic and enjoying the fame (and notoriety) brought him by the super epic which Harry's financing had made possible, the tall lean director owed Aitken a great deal. Now Harry would collect on that debt!

2

The Star Boarders

AS THE TRAIN BEARING GRIFFITH, INCE AND SENNETT ROARED out of Los Angeles, speeding eastward through the dark night enroute to La Junta, Colorado, each man was very much lost in the solitude of his own thoughts. Each had a great deal to gain by agreeing to Harry Aitken's proposition; all had become quite disillusioned and even exasperated with their Mutual affiliation, and as their distribution contracts would expire on September 1, 1915, each realized that now was the time to consider some new avenue of operation.

Of the three, perhaps Griffith should have best understood the man responsible for this trip. In his year and a half with Majestic, Griffith had worked quite closely with Aitken in the production of *The Birth of a Nation*. D. W. appreciated the fact that although Harry had often balked momentarily at the spiraling costs and those unforeseen factors which had caused them (mainly the director's continual enlargement of his theme), he did listen to Griffith's pleas, and reason (as D. W. saw it) had prevailed each time. This degree of freedom from restriction by producers had not been enjoyed by the director in his previous connection and he viewed Aitken as a refreshing breath of life in a cutthroat business.

Slouched in his seat, D. W. stared out the window, watching the occasional lights as they flickered by in the inky darkness and meditating on his career. Even after a decade in the business, it still struck the frustrated playwright as strange that while he could not succeed in his chosen field, fame and now fortune had overtaken him in this topsy-turvy world of make-believe.

Leaving Kentucky with a burning desire for the theatrical world,

Although best remembered for his swashbuckling costume epics of the twenties, Douglas Fairbanks was an exceedingly popular screen star during the World War I period, first at Triangle and then with Paramount. Fairbanks's comedies satirized the contemporary fads and follies of his countrymen and although his athletic hijinks annoyed D. W. Griffith (who thought him better suited for Keystone Comedies), they endeared him to audiences around the world.

Griffith had become a very discouraged individual by 1907. Although he had accumulated some credits as an actor (the last in a touring company with Nance O'Neill), writing had also become very important to him, and in this field he remained unsuccessful. It was this sense of utter frustration, coupled with the urgent physical need to eat, which had sent him to the Edison Company in an effort to sell Edwin Porter some of his ideas for use as movie scripts. Although Porter had rejected the ideas, he offered Griffith work as an actor. The aspiring stage thespian held motion pictures in haughty disdain, as did so many of his contemporaries, but hunger quickly overcame the small semblance of professional pride left. And so, in through the back door came the man destined to become known as the motion picture's greatest creative genius and the most innovative director of the pre-World War I period.

His most notable role at Edison came in *Rescued fom an Eagle's Nest,* in which he saved a doll from the attacks of a stuffed eagle, operated by wires to give the impression of a vicious live bird. But the uncertainty of the stage appeared to have followed Griffith in his new work and so he turned up at Biograph's East 14th Street studio in New York. Given a job as an actor, Griffith soon found that he had made the proper connection this time. Work at the expanding Biograph was steady and he settled down to a sadly resigned but grateful existence as an actor in the "flickers." Soon, he was able to recommend his wife, Linda Arvidson, for parts in various Biograph films, secretly supplementing his income in this way, as his marriage had remained unannounced.

Sufficiently impressing his associates with a feeling for film techniques, Griffith was selected as the director of a new Biograph unit created to expand production in 1908. Reluctantly, the actor moved behind the camera with the understanding that should he not work out in this new capacity, it would not be held against him regarding further Biograph employment as an actor. With this agreement, D. W. set to work and July 1908 saw *The Adventures of Dolly* ready for release.

Although he still failed to regard the artistic potential of the movies in the same light that he had held the legitimate stage, Griffith decided to learn everything possible about the new medium, practicing and experimenting with many different techniques, all of which seemed to be regarded with awe by his fellow workers. Closeups, inter-cutting sequences for suspense, the moving camera—these and many other innovations formed the language of the emerging cinema and were credited to the now-recognized genius of David Wark Griffith.

Over the next five years, Biograph's reputation rose rapidly, ascending almost in direct proportion with Griffith's acceptance at the box-office by the movie-going public. The close relationship between the firm's increasing prestige and profits and its youthful director did not completely escape the attention of Biograph executives. Indeed, it was a point often made by Griffith when personally arguing his case for longer pictures, more production money, less front-office restrictions, etc. But prosperity had created a rose-colored aura which prevented the Biograph powers from seeing reality for what it was; their conservative attitudes toward production and distribution of the product frequently clashed with Griffith's accelerating appreciation of his own worth; bitterness, envy and secrecy toward his employers also grew rapidly.

By the autumn of 1913, D. W. Griffith had compiled quite an impressive record. As a result, his services were desired by many different companies, all willing and able to pay highly for the privilege of claiming him as their own. When Biograph chastised him for producing *Judith of Bethulia* in four reels by taking away his megaphone for a supervisor's chair, the embittered Griffith briefly entertained Adolph Zukor's offer of $1000 weekly to join his Famous Players, a salary several times in excess of that which Biograph had paid him. But Zukor had the reputation of being a somewhat difficult man to work for and Griffith elected to ignore his offer, as well as several others. Instead, he dramatically announced his break with Biograph and joined Harry Aitken's Majestic, surprising the entire industry by his choice.

Majestic had only been able to offer Griffith $300 weekly in salary, but knowing that D. W. realized the value his name would lend to a picture, Aitken had cleverly broken with industry tradition, and as a part of his sales pitch to the much-coveted director offered him a 400-share block of Majestic stock and publicity in the form of screen credits. To Griffith, this was a chance too promising to pass up for just money. Having fought his way through the jungle of executive ignorance that he felt permeated the industry, D. W. could now see the end of a tedious journey and Harry Aitken had appeared to be just the man who could help him reach his long-sought goal of independence.

More and more multi-reel features were taking the place of the single reels which film executives had originally considered to be the longest subjects any movie audience would care to watch. But his creative yearnings (and the success of foreign features in American theaters) told Griffith that the story alone should determine a picture's length, not a front-office dictum. Now Harry Aitken had offered Griffith the very chance of a lifetime—a contract promising him the freedom from executive interference that

Doug Fairbanks and William S. Hart ham it up for the publicity camera. Both would leave Triangle for Paramount and greater fame during 1917. Very popular with audiences, little effort was made to publicize and exploit their Triangle films; Aitken reserved the ballyhoo for his productions with stage stars, which no amount of exploitation could salvage.

his creative talent needed, along with the opportunity to profit directly from his many hours of hard work required by each new film. And so D. W. Griffith joined Majestic and Harry Aitken on October 29, 1913.

A portion of a rare frame enlargement from The Lamb, *Doug Fairbanks's first picture, which opened the Triangle program at the New York Knickerbocker Theatre September 23, 1915, and stole the show, making the athletic stage actor an overnight star. Seena Owen can be seen in the left background.*

Under the terms of his first Majestic contract, Aitken's new director had been allowed to make two special pictures each year on his own, the profits from which were to be split with Harry. Griffith immediately set about supervising the production of Majestic's release schedule of potboilers and planning what he believed would ultimately be recognized as the film's greatest achievement by a fledgling industry within which he had risen from nameless obscurity to a position where the word "genius" was commonly used in describing his talents.

Breaking away from the hypnotic spell created by the incessant clickety-clack of the train as it sped eastward, Griffith got up and walked to the club car, thinking back on the many trials and tribulations which had accompanied his relationship with Harry Aitken over the past 18 months. While D. W. had badly underestimated the cost of *The Clansman,* their first special, Harry had been reasonable in spite of an occasional short-tempered outburst at times, and one way or another Griffith had managed to sell his partner on the need for more and more money. Looking back now, the director couldn't help but chuckle. After investing $40,000 of Mutual's money in the production, Harry had been trapped, with no choice other than to proceed—he had been in no position to stop and shelve the uncompleted film, especially after Mutual's board of directors forced him to pick up the $40,000 from his own pocket. D. W. was no financial wizard, but he did understand the shaky ground upon which Aitken had based his empire, and certain of the success which awaited his completed epic, had willingly pushed Harry out on the limb. The box-office receipts which the film had returned in the past four months were more than enough to vindicate both the genius and self-confidence of D. W. Griffith, and the far-seeing wisdom of the elder Aitken.

II

Sitting in the club car as Griffith walked in, Mack Sennett took a long pull on the big cigar he was smoking and watched the smoke curl upward, nodding hello to the director as he passed by. Too bad, Mack thought, Griffith always had been stuck on himself but the conceit had lately become overbearing in some ways. Thinking back over his past, Sennett concluded that Griffith did have some reason for his self-assurance. Remembering the many long evening walks they had taken when both worked for Biograph, Mack smiled and felt a twinge of gratitude pass over him.

True enough, the "Master" didn't understand or appreciate Mack's comedy any better today than he had at that time; he had always regarded cops and custards as unmitigated nonsense, hardly worthy of the screen. But the director had been encouraging to the ex-boilermaker who was striving, as he was himself, to carve a new career from the films. Trouble with Griffith, Sennett mused, he took himself too seriously. Mack had gone on to greater fame; some were even calling him "The King of Comedy" these days, but he figured he had managed to keep his perspective. Ambition was one thing and it was a fine quality to possess, but life was too short to spend the years looking back at the reflections of past glories. It was also too short to spend working as Griffith did; the fellow ought to have more fun from life than an occasional bottle and girl.

From a unit director at Biograph, Sennett had gone directly to the top as a partner and manager of the Keystone Film Company. August 1912 had been a particularly lucky month for Mack and he owed much of his good fortune to his partners, Ad Kessel and Charlie Baumann. The two bookies-turned-producers had given him the break for which he had waited so long and Mack had made the most of it. Without a doubt, Keystone was the most profitable and best known part of Kessel and Baumann's expanding operation, at least in Mack's mind. Griffith and Tom Ince might get the critical reviews and make a bit of money, but Sennett's Keystone was a household name—the most famous collection of clowns ever to grace the screen—and more than paid its own way.

But Harry Aitken? That was another story. Mack thought back to his early encounters with Mutual's then-president. Aitken had impressed Mack at the time as just another fast-talking country boy (one could hardly fool another) out to flim-flam the city slickers, but Sennett had to admit Harry managed to pull it off. Even though their relationship had been a somewhat stormy one, Mack felt a sense of grudging admiration for the deposed Aitken. Keystone had taken its share of knocks from Harry and Mutual— the distribution outfit paid by the foot for its Keystones, a decided advantage to Mutual, in view of their popularity. Of course, Sennett didn't agree with Mutual's refusal to renegotiate the contract when costs started rising, but after all Harry was bound to the decision of Mutual's directors and was just doing his job as he saw it. The larger return that Mutual stockholders received on their investment, the better job Harry Aitken had done. Mack knew that this line of reasoning, logical as it was, was only a smoke screen which had helped Harry to line his own pockets; Aitken was no different from the rest, including Mack.

Although aware of the realities of life, Mack wondered about this new deal. Before leaving California, Mack had discussed the situation in depth with his studio manager, George W. Stout, and smartly patting the boss's shoulder in a fond goodbye at the station,

Stout reminded Sennett that Mack should demand a new contract for himself. A good man, that Stout, and as capable as they come in an industry hardly noted for efficiency. He was even scrupulously honest, a trait much rarer in the business, and the only man Mack trusted enough to send alone to New York City to represent the Keystone interests in his frequent quarrels with his fast-talking partners.

Mack had been informed by Kessel and Baumann that Keystone's Mutual contract, which expired along with the rest of the New York Motion Picture Company's production and distribution contracts on September 1, 1915, would not be renewed; he had already halted production on his lot as of July 1. Now he was about to join with Ince and Griffith in SIG (Sennett, Ince, Griffith) Pictures, a combine of the NYMP and Aitken forces in what Harry grandly described as the most potent force in the industry. A low-key announcement of SIG had been made to the trade on July 17; all that remained was to sign the contracts. Flattering though the new name might be, something had to be done about it—SIG Pictures left itself wide open for a play on words (SICK Pictures) and Sennett wasn't keen about it; but Aitken had already agreed to change it.

III

Tom Ince had retired early that night; it had been a long day and the Pullman berth looked inviting. Although production had stopped at the studio almost three weeks before, there always seemed to be something to do. When the lot was booming with five or six units shooting every day, maintenance, repairs and all those other little things somehow just got overlooked. But now the situation was well in hand and once this trip was finished, Tom could look forward to several long days of around-the-clock script conferences with Richard V. Spencer, his chief story editor. Ince put in long days, but there never seemed to be enough hours to go around and this trip amounted to his first real vacation in months.

Tom Ince had come a long way since those early days with Carl Laemmle's Imp when he first began directing. Although he still took credit as director quite often, Tom really didn't do too much of the actual work behind the camera anymore. He regarded himself as somewhat of an executive director, supervising the efforts of those directors working under him. Perhaps producer would be a more accurate description, but call it whatever you

The Star Boarders

The original "All-American Boy", Douglas Fairbanks preceded the radio's Jack Armstrong by almost two decades. His super-optimism projected in a breezy, buoyant manner with which everyone could identify and in less than a year, he ranked with William S. Hart as Triangle's most popular favorite. Audiences never seemed to mind the fact that Doug ignored the Horatio Alger version of life, invariably playing the young man of means whose wealth and freedom to do as he pleased allowed him to undertake adventures the average theater patron could only dream about. But that was what it was all about—dreams—and Douglas Fairbanks quickly became a past master at concocting and selling them to a delighted public. But due recognition should be given John Emerson and Anita Loos, who masterminded many of the social satires which set Fairbanks on the path of light comedy.

Here are several representative scenes from film clips of Doug's Triangle features, all 1916 vintage except (7).

(1) Reggie Mixes In

(2) Flirting With Fate

(3) The Americano

(4) The Matrimaniac

(5) His Picture in the Papers

(6) His Picture in the Papers

(7) American Aristocracy *(1917)*

will, Tom often thought, it was still harder work than most people would admit. But his particular organizational talent made the system function, and by 1915 the name of Thomas H. Ince had become one with which to reckon.

Many competitors had tried to emulate his system, but few met with much success. The system was really simplicity in itself but it demanded constant hard work and conscientious attention at all times and this was probably the reason why most who tried to use it failed. For example, Ince demanded and received absolute obedience from everyone on the lot, but most especially from his directors. Once a property had been developed or acquired for filming, his script writers developed a detailed continuity and Tom went over each and every scene with them, approving, disapproving or recommending changes to be incorporated at specific points. The finished product was an extremely detailed shooting script calling out scenes, sets and sequences over which Ince maintained control at all times. Once it met with his complete approval, the script was stamped *Produce this exactly as written* and turned over to a director with an assigned cast, a blueprint ready for production.

The result was an effective assembly line characterized by a high degree of quality control and the individual touch of Thomas H. Ince on each effort. With such a complete script, any director could turn out a good end product, provided he followed his instructions and shot the scenes as they were spelled out. Directors were a funny lot though; many insisted upon their artistic right to film a script as they envisioned it, making changes whenever they disagreed with the writer or to save time or money by cutting corners if the situation presented itself. These directors simply did not last on the Ince lot. Once the footage was shot, Ince had chosen the rushes personally and edited them into a finished picture himself. With such complete control over every aspect of production, he was able to turn out better pictures than his competitors while still keeping costs within reason. Of late, however, Tom just simply hadn't been able to find time to do all of the required editing personally and recently he had taken to supervising the cutters much as he did the directors.

Ince's name had not always evoked the respect it carried in 1915. Only four years before, Ince had joined Kessel and Baumann's New York Motion Picture Company at a salary of $125 weekly, a rather substantial increase over what Imp had been paying him.

Tom had left immediately for the West Coast with Raymond Smallwood as his cameraman and Ethel Grandin as leading lady to assume occupancy of the dilapidated structure at Edendale which Kessel and Baumann glowingly referred to as a studio. His mission was simple—to send back a sufficient number of western pictures for release as Bison films, the brand with which Kessel and Baumann had opened business in 1909.

The market had been surfeited with cowboy and Indian pictures in the 1909-12 period, so much so that representatives of various Indian tribes around the country registered a protest with the Bureau of Indian Affairs about their "screen image." But Tom Ince's westerns had been different from the very beginning—his played men, both red and white, against the elements of nature, and Tom's uncanny sense of the visual led to sweeping panoramas of the plains and mountains. In Ince westerns, the red man was portrayed as a majestic figure inevitably tinged with the tragic. Once he had acquired the services of the Miller Brothers 101 Ranch Wild West Show for use in the off-season, the Bison films began to make Tom Ince's reputation.

Essentially a businessman who had systematized production on the lot, Ince kept it functioning at peak efficiency by holding a tight rein on everything that was done. Although not a creative figure in the mold of Griffith, Ince did have certain talents that many of his contemporaries lacked. The application of these had led to his nickname, "The Aesop of Inceville." His power to visualize a script was unusually keen and combined with a narrative flair to make Ince films flow smoothly from start to finish. Placing a heavy emphasis on the story, Tom exercised a ruthlessness almost unknown in the business at the time in paring his footage to the bone. Anything which failed to advance the plot was cut out, leaving a picture which made its point effectively.[1]

The Ince touch thus consisted of a tight dramatic structure, a clean-cut style and directness in story approach. One of the first

---

[1] This preoccupation with the story line could be traced back to the beginning of Ince's career as a director. While with Imp, he made a number of single-reel pictures with Mary Pickford and Owen Moore and one of these, *Artful Kate,* is an excellent example of the Ince use of a story.

Basically the story of two lovers separated by a naval tour of duty in Havana, the picture told of Mary, who went to Cuba on vacation, posed as a Spanish senorita to test Owen's love and broke him down. Upon his return to Mary, Owen vowed he had remained true, only to register profound shock and dismay when presented with the evidence of his indiscretion. But all was forgiven as the reel closed on this remarkably sparse story which had moved at a lightning pace.

film makers to use psychologically motivated themes, he pitted his characters against the impersonal and unpredictable manifestations of nature, often in an atmosphere of foreboding despair. It was not uncommon for his films to omit the artificial happy endings characteristic of the times, leaving the audience deep in tragedy as the next film flashed on the screen. As a result, Ince's films were hailed for their emotional impact and profound realism. While he is probably best remembered today for his William S. Hart westerns of the 1914-15 period (for which Hart was really due more credit than Tom), they were not completely representative of the best of Ince; one has to look to subjects like *The Drummer of the Eighth, In the Tennessee Hills* and *In the Switch Tower* to find the real Ince touch.[2] Because of the unique system under which he functioned, Tom's name had appeared on the majority of the films which came from the assembly line, giving rise to a reputation for productivity unmatched by other directors of the time. He would keep it that way.

---

[2] *The Drummer of the Eighth* was a Civil War picture in which the proud parents prepared a grand welcome for their young hero only to open the door and find a casket; *In the Tennessee Hills* closes as the hero, who had killed a man in an argument, is saved from hanging and rides into hiding; *In the Switch Tower* told the story of a neglectful father sent to prison for a barroom brawl. Paroled, he returns to save his son, who thought him dead, without identifying himself.

3

A One Night Stand

OVER DINNER WITH J. J. MCCARTHY[1] THAT NIGHT, HARRY AITKEN found himself unable to contain his absolute delight. Safely locked away in a battered black briefcase were contracts bearing the signatures of Kessel and Baumann, Griffith, Sennett and Ince. Once he returned to New York and delivered the documents into the hands of Smithers and Company, the Triangle Film Corporation would become a reality. July 20 in La Junta had been a hot day, with the heat of the discussion often reaching the temperature outside the Harvey House, but in spite of several issues of contention regarding salaries, percentages and a corporate name, everyone had basically agreed with Aitken—the concept of Triangle possessed the potential to wrest control of the growing industry away from the Zukors and Laemmles—and signed the agreements.

Absolutely convinced that the necessary signatures would be forthcoming with a minimum of difficulty, Harry had previously arranged for a Certificate of Incorporation to be filed in Richmond, Virginia, on July 19. On that date, the Triangle Film Corporation officially came into existence, capitalized at a minimum par value of $1000 and a maximum of $5 million, to be divided into shares with a par value of $5.00 each. While the State of Delaware had perhaps the most liberal corporation regulations in the country, Aitken had deliberately chosen Virginia for a very good reason. News traveled fast in the motion picture world and Harry didn't

---

[1] McCarthy had directed the twelve *Birth of a Nation* roadshow companies. Chosen for the job because of his previous success in exploiting motion pictures in Philadelphia under heavy fire from the forces of censorship, McCarthy ran interference for Aitken and Griffith in the dozens of legal actions, street demonstrations and political battles involved with the film's exhibition and was now a trusted associate of Aitken and close advisor on matters of exploitation.

want to tip his hand to Freuler and the rest of the industry. Although he had often been seen in the company of various financiers, this was a normal association for the now-deposed promoter whose Mutual organization had made a strong bid to replace the Patents Trust as the source of Carl Laemmle's migraine headaches in 1912-14. To insure further that the veil of secrecy he had drawn around his future activities would not be inadvertently parted by some snooping individual, Harry had arranged for the incorporation papers to be filed by one Robert E. Peyton, Jr., of Richmond, naming Peyton, William W. Beverley and Howard K. Wood as officers and directors of the corporation. At the appropriate moment, Peyton and company would hand the reins over to Aitken and associates, and then fade quickly into the dark obscurity of time.

Aitken's plan was a daring one—the establishment of an organization to produce, distribute and exhibit films—a horizontal consolidation of the business revolving around the three men who were probably the most talented producers in the industry at the time. Each one became a vice-president of Triangle, as did Kessel and Baumann, and thus were entitled to hold Triangle stock while still producing and drawing salaries from their individual companies, Majestic, Keystone or the New York Motion Picture Company. Triangle would reimburse the producing companies for their immediate negative costs and furnish the operating capital on a draw basis. Through its own exchange system Triangle would then distribute all pictures made by the three producers to theaters holding Triangle contracts, withholding 35 percent of gross receipts for its distribution service and returning the remaining 65 percent minus other Triangle operating expenses to the producing companies in the form of credits to their drawing accounts.

Theaters without Triangle contracts would not be allowed to rent Triangle pictures under any circumstances, thus removing one source of income from the corporate coffers, but also doing away with cyclical variations in sales and income. Contracting customers in effect held Triangle franchises which assured them that they would not be in competition with every other theater in their area and tended to make each one a prestige house by virtue of its Triangle monopoly.

Although capitalized to do so, Triangle would not actually produce pictures unless business became so great that its three producers could not keep up with the demand. The 65 percent would

Douglas Fairbanks returns to Hollywood from the East Coast. His light comic portrayals of the irresponsible young American male who rose to whatever the occasion demanded rapidly won him a large following and he proved to be one of Triangle's biggest stars.

finance production, pay overhead, and in addition return a handsome profit over and above costs. Triangle-owned showcase theaters, strategically located in major cities across the nation, would pay the Triangle exchanges the same rental fee as any comparable theater, but have the right to first-run exhibition in their city. As a result, it was anticipated that the theater chain could look forward to enjoying a brisk and highly profitable business.

As the Triangle exchange system was to be the key to an efficient distribution of the programs, both to Triangle theaters and Triangle contractors, it was imperative that they be properly structured and operated. To undertake this task, Aitken hired J. R. Naulty, formerly the head of distribution for General Film, the dying Patent Trust's exchange arm. Naulty's task was to organize a nationwide network, but the job contained an interesting twist. His exchanges were to handle *only* the Triangle program, and as

An inveterate "mugger," Ford Sterling had been with Sennett from the beginning, but unlike other comics on the lot, he had a habit of leaving Keystone to work on his own or for other comedy producers. The fact that Sennett always took him back was an indication of their close relationship, as Sennett regarded loyalty from his comedians as a prerequisite for employment equal to talent. Sterling's fame was passing him by when Stars and Bars *(1917) was released and he would soon become a victim of his own primitive comedy style. Mae Emory was the lady.*

it was envisioned this would consist of two features, one each from Griffith and Ince, and two comedies from Sennett. There would be a new program every week, with theaters playing one feature and comedy for the first half of the week and replacing them at

Al St. John was Roscoe Arbuckle's nephew but Al's ability to ride a trick bicycle was far more decisive in Sennett's decision to hire him. St. John had a long and unimportant career with Sennett as a supporting comic and his few starring roles were mainly in the Triangle Comedies which Aitken produced in 1916–17 using Sennett's idle comics. A Self-Made Hero with Vera Steadman was one made in 1916 before Al left to join Arbuckle in his Paramount comedies of 1917.

mid-week with the other half of the Triangle package. Compared to the competition's exchange systems, which handled at least a dozen or more new films weekly, this scheme was the ultimate in simplicity. Booking difficulties due to differing combinations would be eliminated altogether. All that would really be required was a sufficient quantity of each program to meet the demands of scheduling among the Triangle contractors.

The Triangle showcase theater circuit was Aitken's private scheme, but it also made sense to his partners. Triangle's own theaters would operate at premium prices; Aitken's experience with *The Birth of a Nation* had already proven to him that there was a public willing to pay a minimum of $2.00 per seat to see outstanding pictures. Showcase seats would thus range between $2.00 and $3.00 each. Triangle would attempt to secure the most prestigious location in each major city, skimming the cream directly into company coffers before general release to Triangle contract theaters located in the same city, which paid the standard rental fee. While the theater network was envisioned as containing no more than a half-dozen houses, this was the most expensive part of Triangle's projected plan and recognized by all as such. Theaters of the desired quality and location could not be leased or built cheaply and so initially only two theaters were acquired, both on a lease arrangement.

A fine old theater temporarily made over for motion pictures, New York's Knickerbocker Theatre on Broadway and 38th Street, was subleased for $65,000 from Klaw and Erlanger and the Charles Frohman Company for a one-year period, beginning in early August 1915. The Studebaker in Chicago was also leased at the same time. Planning to premiere the Triangle program at the Knickerbocker on September 23, Aitken had spent a month renovating and decorating the house for its new role.

Caught up in the rhetoric of his own sales pitch, Harry grandly announced to the world at large that Triangle pictures would soon supplant the spoken drama, with the Triangle movie palaces (or, as he preferred to call them, Theatres of Science and Artifice) quickly becoming the cultural centers of each major city. The Triangle contract clients would bring enlightenment to the hinterlands in a cultural explosion the likes of which could only be imagined. It should be recorded that Harry Aitken was not the first nor the last of a long line of motion picture impresarios whose belief in their product would later force them to swallow the bitter hemlock which accompanies disaster.

General release of Triangle's first program across the nation was announced for October 15, followed weekly by a new program.

Mack Swain was the rare comedian who could also turn in a fine dramatic performance. Before joining Keystone, he had his own stock company in Salt Lake City. Famed as the "Ambrose" of Keystone days, Swain was another of the Sennett regulars whose career was briefly eclipsed when the stage comics first arrived on the lot. Their failure to produce soon brought Swain back into the picture, more valuable than ever, in comedies like Ambrose's Cup of Woe *(1916) with Mae Emory and Paul Jacobs.*

This schedule gave Triangle's three producers about eleven weeks to gear up their production, providing a backlog for the variety of unexpected contingencies that could arise—poor weather, a studio destroyed by fire, laboratory problems, etc. It also meant that the new Triangle program would not be in conflict with the final Griffith, Ince and Sennett releases which completed their obligation to Mutual. Fortunately, each of the producers possessed a small quantity of pictures which were produced while under contract for Mutual distribution but had not been needed to fulfill their obligations. As Mutual had bought their product outright, paying a specified sum per foot for each ordered print, there was no prior claim against these films. If necessary, they could be and were used as Triangle pictures.

Production began in earnest as soon as Griffith, Ince and Sennett returned to California. Already, the first contingent of Triangle's

Another scene from Ambrose's Cup of Woe *(1916), with Mae Emory, Paul Jacobs and comedian Mack Swain, whose blustering comic portrayals were occasionally touched with a pathos unknown in Sennett's comedies, and a talent that brought him a role in Chaplin's* The Gold Rush *(1925), which critics still agree remains one of the finest sequences in visual comedy. The young artist is more familiar to Laurel and Hardy fans of the late twenties and to devotees of the two-reel comedy short subjects in the thirties as that master of the "slow-burn," Edgar Kennedy.*

additional player roster had started flooding to the West Coast. To Harry Aitken, this was the most important asset and the one that would lift Triangle to the heights of the motion picture industry. Drawing from the stage for his material, Harry envisioned the creation of an entirely new spectrum of movie stars and so hired Arthur Klein, a theatrical agent, to help entice notable talent at wages ranging from $1000 to $2500 weekly.

This was not an original idea with Aitken—it had been tried by Adolph Zukor in 1912-14 and found wanting. Learning the hard (and expensive) way that patrons preferred to create their own stars, Zukor had quickly been forced to abandon the idea as unprofitable. Why Aitken thought the situation had changed materially is still a mystery, unless he thought that times had changed considerably; but he was successful in convincing both his backers and associates (except Mack Sennett) that the public would indeed accept Broadway stars in extravagantly mounted productions, a mistake that ultimately played a measurable role in Triangle's hasty demise.

The initial Triangle roster included Billie Burke, Mary Boland, Julia Dean, Bessie Barriscale, De Wolf Hopper, Raymond Hitchcock, Sam Bernard, Eddie Foy, Weber and Fields, H. B. Warner, Dustin Farnum, Frank Keenan, Hale Hamilton, Williard Mack, Harry Woodruff, Forrest Winant, Orrin Johnson, Maurice Farkoa, Louise Dresser, House Peters, Jane Grey, William Desmond and Douglas Fairbanks, in addition to those players who had been retained from the Keystone, Majestic-Reliance and NYMP forces.

Triangle's production facilities were adequate at the outset but no one denied that expansion and updating would be required almost immediately if its promises to exhibitors were to be kept. While Griffith was given approximately 15,000 square feet of production space, enough to house his fifteen directors at work, Ince's facilities at Inceville in the Santa Ynez canyon contained a capacity of over 50,000 square feet. Sennett's Edendale lot was a ramshackle affair, affectionately nicknamed "The Pig Sty" in recognition of its state of disrepair. Expansion had taken place on this old Bison lot but much of it had been of wood frame construction erected in a hurry and Mack set his sights on quickly replacing as much as he could with modern concrete buildings. Triangle had leased two floors of office space in New York City's new Brokaw Building, but moved into Kessel and Baumann's offices located in the Longacre Building until its new accommodations were ready. By early September, several pictures had been completed under the Triangle aegis and Harry Aitken had selected his choices for the first program.

II

Remembering the agonizing process of choosing the initial pictures to be shown, Harry was relieved to read the favorable trade reviews which followed opening night. But reviewers outside the industry were not so uniformly enthusiastic about Triangle's achievements. Typical of the attitude of many, the staid *New York Times* commented on the pictures Aitken had selected by saying, "Each is an example of nicely accomplished motion picture photography, no one of them reveals anything amazing or unprecedented in the development of this now hugely popular form of entertainment. Anyone who went to the Knickerbocker last evening looking for that must have come away disappointed.

"But anyone who goes with a movie mind will find at least one picture that is an exceedingly good sample of the best work now being done for the screen and will meet a new movie actor who is certain to build an enormous following in that considerable multitude which is possessed of a passion for the cinema."[2] And in this judgment, the collective opinion of trade and non-trade reviewers was in collective agreement: Douglas Fairbanks was an instant success.

No one had planned it that way. Everyone connected with Triangle had fully expected Dustin Farnum (who had left his promising stage career in 1914 to star in Bosworth Pictures) to carry the day with his role in *The Iron Strain*. This was especially true of Griffith, who had supervised Christy Cabanne's direction of *The Lamb*, cringing all the while at the thought of Fairbanks. But writing for *The Moving Picture World,* Louis Reeves Harrison called Fairbanks ". . . a comedian who wins through interesting personality and delightful characterizations, a decided relief from the raw crudities of acrobatic clowns . . . he holds the eye so strongly and without apparent effort, that he is the whole play from beginning to end."[3] *The New York Times* commented, "His engaging personality easily and undeniably registers—as the film folk say. He is amusing, graphic, humorous, effortless. . . ."[4]

[2] *The New York Times,* September 24, 1915, p. 11.
[3] *The Moving Picture World,* October 9, 1915, p. 233.
[4] *The New York Times,* September 24, 1915, p. 11.

Triangle had transformed a Broadway actor into a new movie star overnight, much to Griffith's chagrin. But an immediate second thought told him that Harry Aitken's aim to create new stars had hit target dead center; Douglas Fairbanks *had been* an unknown quantity in the eyes of the reviewers and patrons. But D. W. had no way of knowing that such a fortunate stroke of luck would not happen to Triangle again.

A personable and engaging fellow whose *joie de vivre* had found an outlet on the stage, Douglas Fairbanks was a reasonably well-known Broadway actor[5] who had been courted somewhat earlier by Daniel Frohman with an offer to enter motion pictures. Fairbanks had gone so far as actually to make a screen test for Famous Players, but nothing had developed as a result. In his *A Million and One Nights,* Terry Ramsaye credits Kessel and Baumann with masterminding Doug's capitulation to Triangle over lunch at the Knickerbocker Grill, but it was Harry Aitken who signed Fairbanks to a three-year contract at $2000 weekly the first year, $2500 the second and $3000 the third, a staggering sum for an unknown quantity.

When word reached Griffith by telegram from New York that Fairbanks was enroute to Los Angeles, the director called a hurried consultation with Frank Woods and Mary O'Connor of his scenario department. Together, they quickly adapted the story line of Fairbanks' stage hit, *The New Henrietta,* for his first picture. Entitled *The Lamb,* it went to the screen bearing a writing credit to Granville Warwick, Griffith's screen-writing pseudonym. Fairbanks had reported to the Fine Arts studio, only to discover within a few days that Griffith was less than enthusiastic about his presence. Although his contract specifically called for Griffith to direct, or closely supervise the direction of his pictures, Fairbanks soon found that "The Master" was far too busy and not at all interested in him or his screen career. The filming of *The Lamb* cast the mold for their relationship, which would grow progressively worse as time went by. Believing that movies should move, Doug had turned his ebullient spirit loose before the camera, causing Griffith to caustically suggest that if "The Jumping Jack" would only hop, skip and jump over to Sennett's comedy lot, he was certain Fairbanks would find a more suitable home there. Time would prove

---

[5] His acting career had begun in 1901 at Ford's Theatre in Baltimore with a role in *Richelieu,* a portrayal which eventually led to a seven-year contract with William A. Brady.

Madcap Mabel Normand in a studio gag shot. Often called the female Chaplin of the screen, Mabel was undoubtedly its most gifted comedienne. Her Keystone and Triangle years were mainly custard pies and pratfalls until 1916 brought her the opportunity to do Mickey for her own company, financed by Sennett with Kessel and Baumann. While fans adored the little comedienne, nicknaming her "Keystone Mabel," her most creative work came in the early twenties.

Douglas Fairbanks to be one of the outstanding personalities of the silent screen, but Griffith never relented one inch publicly in his opinion, nor did he ever make an effort to claim a share of the credit, as so many other directors would have done; while he might have been many other things, D. W. Griffith was never a hypocrite.

Ince's offering of *The Iron Strain* was C. Gardner Sullivan's variation on the old and oft-used story of a vigorous western hero and his relationship with a cultured but sickly city girl. Forcing her to marry him, Farnum nursed her back to health, but not until the town vamp returned would she admit her love for her husband. As the heroine, Enid Markey was required to project a character transformation in several gradual stages from hate to love and in doing so, stole the show right from under Farnum's experienced nose.

Mack Sennett's contribution to Triangle's opening acclaim was *My Valet,* a four-reel subject taken from an old reliable stage comedy. Newcomer Raymond Hitchcock carried the burden as lead, supported by Mabel Normand, Fred Mace and Sennett himself. Playing against Mace's 1912 form of villainy and Sennett's stilted performance, Hitchcock looked rather good by comparison. By this time, both Sennett and Keystone were well on their way to becoming a legend (thanks to Mack's able press agents) and trade reviewers tended to pull their punches as a result. But many outside the industry did not fail to point out that Hitchcock seemed unable to "project" from the movie screen as he had on the stage, coming across to screen audiences as a cold personality. On this basis, they questioned the suitability of Triangle's new $2000-a-week comic. Within a few months, so would Sennett.

But by any yardstick, the Triangle enterprise acquitted itself admirably on premiere night and appeared to be heading for great success. Aitken, his partners and backers all agreed on this and looked forward with anticipation to a rosy future in their effort to overwhelm the already established moguls of the motion picture world.[6] Even had they realized it, no one connected with Triangle would have admitted that almost concurrent with its launching, a kind of dry rot was set in motion.

---

[6] Famous Players had just suffered an unexpected reverse resulting from a fire which destroyed its 26th Street studio in New York. Of the eleven feature negatives in the vault ready for release printing, only one survived the intense heat intact. The financial loss was estimated at $500,000 and temporarily removed much of the creative competition which Triangle was to face.

4

The Three-Must-Get-Theres

SETTLING BACK AGAINST THE LIMOUSINE'S SOFT CUSHIONED SEAT, Thomas Harper Ince smiled at his wife and then looked through the window at the dull blackness outside as the chauffeur gently eased the car into motion; he much preferred the company of Dorothy Dalton, but protocol demanded that Mrs. Ince accompany him to the gala occasion which would mark this New Year's Eve of 1916. The new Culver City studio was to be formally dedicated in a few hours and Ince found it hard to hold back a wave of excitement. Shrewd businessman that he was, Tom realized that the new studio was a grand coup. What other producer in the business could boast of a twelve-acre studio lot, complete with brand new concrete buildings and a 165-foot electrically lighted stage area? Especially when Ince held the deed and NYMP had paid for the studio! The only thing the competition had to offer was Universal City, which had just opened a few months before, but Tom was convinced that he would soon out-Laemmle his old boss. The past was prelude; tonight was really just the beginning!

It had been a long journey—that trip from nowhere which had ended in a home at 5928 Franklin Street in Hollywood, where he could slip off his shoes, relax and think about the old days when the routine was to pack his bag in time to catch a train which would carry him to the next small town and another one night stand. Of course, the fame and fortune he had accumulated along the way made it difficult to spend his little free time at home and relax. He was living an entirely different life now, and girls and glamor had replaced home and hearth for Tom. At any rate, he did appreciate the sense of belonging which his home gave; no matter how far you went in this world, you really couldn't outrun or escape

Louise Fazenda, Harry Booker and Charlie Murray in a scene from one of their "Maggie" comedies of 1917. Murray, a long-time veteran of the stage who also entered movies with Biograph, developed a following during his Triangle years which would make him Sennett's leading comic in the early twenties.

Louise Fazenda signs for a telegram in His Precious Life *(1917), while Slim Summerville waits patiently. Miss Fazenda was a genuine comic talent who did not have to rely upon pratfalls or outrageous "mugging" at the camera to create her laughs and became one of the twenties' most beloved comediennes.*

Claire Anderson, one of the dependable and popular Triangle actresses whose popularity with audiences was never touched by the magic of stardom.

your past, even though Tom was making a good attempt at trying to.

Chuckling softly to himself, Tom's thoughts slid back to 1910 and his first meeting with Carl Laemmle. Both men had been striving hard in those days; Laemmle to avoid the ever-present spectre of bankruptcy and Ince simply to eat. Laemmle having proven a sharp thorn in its sensitive side, the Patents Trust have put a great deal of pressure on the wily little German dry goods merchant who dared to challenge it. Ince, although born of show business parents, had struggled for success in the theatrical world, but by the time he was 29, Tom had come to the realization that what he wanted and needed was not forthcoming from the stage. And what he had needed most of all that September day five years ago had been money.

It was Ince's idea that he should never associate with less than the best which the theatrical world had to offer and as a result, the young actor had limited himself as to the companies with which he would work, feeling it better to be a servant with a good touring company than a leading man with those he considered to be inferior. Coupled with this attitude, his rather pudgy build restricted the roles he was offered and a man couldn't go through life playing only juveniles. Up to that time, Tom reflected, he had never even considered moving pictures, feeling that those actors who had made the move were the riffraff of the theatrical world and the stage was better off for their absence.

But money had its own sense of urgency and while Ince hadn't minded his low earnings and many periods of unemployment before, there was now a son to be considered and the actor felt that his wife and child should not be asked to suffer for his professional inadequacies. Thus it was that September 1910 found him "at liberty" once again, on his way home to the little uptown flat to face an $8.00 rent bill with only $10.00 in his pocket. It was in this discouraging circumstance that he had happened across a former acquaintance, one whom Tom considered to be a mediocre actor but whose current financial condition included one of the largest limousines Ince had seen close up for a long time. A few minutes of idle chatter served both to pass the time of day and convince Tom that perhaps movies were the answer to his plight. Bidding the benefactor of his morale goodbye, Tom hustled across town to the Imp studio and applied for a job. His work started the next day and was good for a $5.00 bill each and every working day—affluence at last!

The hard-working actor had learned quickly and soon moved to Biograph, but only for a week. Returning to Imp, Ince was elevated to the position of director and shortly took a company to Cuba. Laemmle had stolen "Little Mary" Pickford from under the nose of Biograph and the Trust was after his scalp. The one answer seemed to be to leave the country and Cuba was chosen as the destination. Tom had spent several months there, turning out single reel dramas with Mary and her husband Owen Moore as fast as the camera could grind the scripts through under the pressure of a relentless release schedule which was constantly in danger of overtaking him. Appalled at the average motion picture which Imp (as well as the Trust) put on the screen, Ince had decided that quality control was a desirable feature lacking in the business. In addition, his professional pride told him that a reputation could be made easily in a field overcrowded by those contented with "quick and dirty" productions. And so the new director devoted his spare hours to scripting, editing and development of the production system for which he was now famous. Cuba had served as his school, the training ground which had prepared him for the big move to the New York Motion Picture Company in 1911.

His association with Kessel and Baumann had been the turning point in Tom's career. Having sent Ince West and eager to avail themselves of every possible option they encountered, the New York Motion Picture Company's executives had approved their new director's idea of hiring the Miller Brothers 101 Ranch Show and Tom had been off and running from that point. Limiting himself to the field of westerns and Civil War pictures, Ince had turned out films under the Bison 101 and later, the Kay Bee banner, which proved to be immensely successful with exhibitors. From that point on, it had been almost continuous expansion.

As the limousine turned onto Washington Boulevard and neared the entrance to the new studio, Tom's thoughts returned to the present and the new studio—the latest symbol of his success. Situated in the new and rapidly growing community of Culver City, the lot would include eight stages 60 by 150 feet. Four were completed and in use now; the other four would soon be finished. While the new administration building, which housed both the executive offices and the scenario department, was not yet finished, the property rooms, carpenter and plumbing shops, restaurant, commissary, garages and most of the 300 player dressing rooms were ready for occupancy. And Kessel and Baumann had just agreed to purchase an adjoining lot of 31 acres, providing space for filming exteriors without sending the crews to Inceville or Santa Monica.

Although the original idea had been to abandon both older facilities, Tom had now decided not to give them up; added to the new studio, they gave him almost unlimited potential for filming Triangle pictures. Situated on the slopes of the entrance to Santa Ynez Canyon, Inceville had been his home away from home since the fall of 1911. The plant resembled many of the other early studios—it sprawled in ungainly confusion as wood frame buildings had been hastily constructed to meet the needs of Tom's ever-expanding empire. The two original stages (both 50 by 80 feet) were now used as auxiliary facilities, supporting the newer main stage 175 by 220 feet in size. But these were all dwarfed by the recently-added glass-enclosed 160 by 360 foot stage. With the many supporting buildings required on a studio lot, Inceville had become a sprawling ramshackle affair. The permanent sets—a

Spanish mission, Dutch, Irish, Japanese and Canadian villages, an East Indian street and Sioux camp—were supplemented by 18,000 acres of landscape which possessed an almost inexhaustible potential for natural settings to support the sets.

The logistics of such growth had been almost unbelievable. Inceville and the Santa Monica ranch employed 600 people and at least another 300 would be required to man the new half-million dollar studio. Five years before, Ince had been without a job—now almost a thousand employees looked to him for a living. Yes, it had been quite a worthwhile experience, leading him from the rented cold water flat in New York to his own luxurious nine-room house in California, exquisitely furnished in the decor of Louis XIV, and whose large Roman pool situated under a pergola was bordered by palms, mutely testifying to the affluence of its owner.

It was a few minutes before nine when the limousine slowed down to turn into the studio entrance and Tom's thoughts leaped ahead to the evening's festivities, arranged by his business manager, Edward Allen. Over 500 guests had been invited to celebrate the occasion. The Grand March would be led by the Inces at midnight, followed by a pantomime sketch illustrating the death of the old year (played by Walt Whitman) and the birth of 1916 (portrayed by little Thelma Salter). As Tom helped his wife step from the limousine, the faint smile of a man who knows the wisdom of past decisions crossed his parted lips.

One other thought passed quickly through Tom Ince's mind as they went up the steps and inside to meet his guests. After more than a year in planning, Tom's greatest achievement was about ready to unveil. He had decided at the moment Griffith's *The Birth of a Nation* had proved successful that a massive feature effort was both desirable and necessary. Calling in C. Gardner Sullivan, Ince had explained what was going through his mind as best he could to his top scenario writer. A former newspaperman, an excellent craftsman of screen scripts and sometime crutch for the busy producer to lean on, Sullivan was equally excited about the prospects of doing an epic and set to work almost immediately on a story line which would reflect the ideas he and Tom had discussed.

The more that Ince had thought about the idea, the more it had appealed to him—an exposure of what the horrors of war did to humanity—a pacifist plea for the peace and tranquility Europe had thrown to the wind in its desperate attempt to realign the old

Starting with Griffith in 1909, Marguerite Marsh paved the way to the screen for her younger sister Mae and saw her own career stymied in films like The Price of Power *(Fine Arts, 1916), shown here with Clyde Hopkins. Marguerite spent her last screen years in independent pictures after starring in a 1919 serial for Oliver Films.*

order. Ince's extremely idealistic nature, somewhat of a paradox in the successful businessman of the period, was curiously mixed with an equal measure of patriotism, a personal feeling reflected time after time in his films. Although a showman first and last, and one who knew the value of tear-jerking clichés to box-office receipts, Ince had managed to combine his own personal feelings with his one goal in life—making movies that made money. The excitement Tom felt for this film convinced him that it would make money by the baskets, no question about it; the public reaction to Vitagraph's *The Battle Cry of Peace* and other pro-war propaganda had been immensely profitable but Ince's intuition told him that there was a huge unexploited market for pacifism; this was his chance to mine the deep anti-war sentiment in the country.

Ground had been broken in the hills of Inceville during May 1915 for a costly ($35,000) set representing the mythical kingdom of Wredpryd in which the action was to center. The construction had taken six months, 600,000 feet of lumber, $4000 of window glass, over 100 tons of cement and plaster, with uncounted trees, shrubbery and lamp posts dotting the 6½ acre set. No title had yet been given the super-spectacle at this point, but all moviedom knew that "The Aesop of Inceville" had embarked on a gigantic venture and referred to it as Ince's "big picture."

Shooting began in June with Herschel Mayall leading the cast and supported by other Ince regulars—Howard Hickman, J. Frank Burke, Lola May, Ethel Ulman and J. Barney Sherry. Under Ince's close supervision, Raymond B. West had directed the photography of 121,000 feet of negatives (including retakes). That production would now be finished within the week had not escaped Ince's notice. Beginning in January, Tom would have to work nights supervising the cutting of the footage into a film of about eleven reels. As soon as editing was completed, Victor Schert-

The hypocrisy and bigotry of formal religion was attacked in Martha's Vindication *(Fine Arts, 1916), with Seena Owen and Ralph Lewis. Norma Talmadge was also featured in this powerful entry.*

zinger would begin scoring the accompanying music. Ince's "big picture" would then be titled and released to the public for its seal of approval—box-office cash. Tom Ince had no doubts—it would top anything he had done to date and with the country's mood, should earn as much as had any of Griffith's "masterpieces." It might even make his critics happy too.

II

D. W. hadn't paid too much attention to Ince and his picture—"The Belasco of the Screen" was too engrossed with his own answer to *The Birth of a Nation* and his critics. Hurt, puzzled and bewildered over the storm of controversy which swirled around his first spectacle film, Griffith had at first lashed back at his critics, using pamphlets, newspaper interviews and lectures to combat what he felt to be injustice, ignorance and jealousy. But these only added fuel to the fire, and as the controversy grew hotter and hotter D. W. decided to answer his critics in the way which one would expect of any true artist of the screen—he picked up his megaphone to put his definitive reply on film.

Coupled with this defensive posture was an awareness that daily supervision of Triangle's program pictures would never sustain the recognition he had achieved as a major innovator in the industry. Griffith realized that it had taken *The Birth of a Nation* to focus the spotlight of attention upon him and now everyone was waiting with anticipation to see how he would top this phenomenal success. Speaking with Harry Aitken, Griffith had suggested that he begin work on the next super picture allowed under his contract, expanding the theme of *The Mother and the Law* to epic proportions.[1]

By this time, Harry had a good feeling for the way in which Griffith's mind worked and cut in to ask the cost of the proposed venture. Griffith's reply was a modest shrug of his shoulders. At this point, Aitken had politely suggested that D. W. have his pulse and temperature checked—the fever was apparently very high. *The Birth of a Nation* had cost over $120,000 to produce and now Griffith was shrugging his shoulders again. As D. W. saw it, Harry's cost to participate should be one-half, but with Griffith's fine knack for underestimating the real cost, no one could predict

---

[1] A Reliance-Majestic feature produced while at Mutual but not yet released. Based on the Stielow case, *The Mother and the Law* involved the killing of 19 employees by a chemical manufacturer's hired hoodlums during a strike for higher pay. Griffith used this basic story line as a hinge for his realistic study of economic oppression and slum life, a theme often touched upon briefly by the movies.

how much above this original estimate the final figure would be. But eventually, a compromise was arrived at and Harry and Roy Aitken agreed to underwrite the new project for an amount giving them a quarter interest, with production to be undertaken by the Wark Producing Company, Griffith's own firm.

Deciding upon the concept of parallel stories[2] as a device to trace the history of intolerance through the ages, D. W. established a need for a life-size replica of ancient Babylon, and huge sets with 90-foot high walls began to rise on the vacant lot opposite the Fine Arts studio on Sunset Boulevard. Assuming gigantic proportions almost from the beginning, the production logistics soon became unbelievable and found Griffith supervising up to 28 assistant directors at times, as several thousand extras were put through their paces for Billy Bitzer's nine cameras. When the battle scenes were filmed, it was a chaos such as Hollywood had never before seen—1000 men defended the walls as 2000 more on foot and in chariots assaulted the city with paper arrows and papier-maché boulders. Dr. Robert Hackett supervised medical services, treating over 300 injuries on the set, in addition to dispatching over 60 people to the hospital. Proving to be a major nuisance, interested spectators pushed and tripped over each other for a better view, agreeing that even if Griffith had used no film in the cameras, the resulting circus had indeed topped *The Birth of a Nation*.

It was a pity that audiences across the nation would not agree with this judgment when the film was finally released. Caught up completely with the enormity of what he was doing, Griffith had failed to take into account the average moviegoer of the time. While the program pictures which his directoral staff were turning out across the way at the studio left something to be desired from the audiences' standpoint, D. W.'s effort to provide entertainment for those who bought his theater tickets would stray even further from the mainstream, a fact which had eluded Griffith's usually keen grasp in his anxiety to preach. Had he only bothered to analyze the production of the Fine Arts studio and its public reception, "The Master" would have seen the other side of the coin. But no matter; Griffith was no longer producing entertainment—this was to be a moral lesson.

---

[2] Which was really an amplification of the techniques Griffith had used in his earlier *Judith of Bethulia* (1913). The thematic relationship of four separate stories had been a rather intriguing approach favored by Griffith in several subsequent pictures (like *The Escape*, 1914) prior to its culmination in *Intolerance*.

His grandstand play would fail and fail magnificently, but D. W. was unaware of this as he fought with investors for additional capital, argued at length with Harry for not backing the venture with more of his own (and some of Triangle's) money and eventually agreeing to buy out everyone who had contributed. Tapping the rich lode provided by his share of *The Birth of a Nation*, Griffith would pour an immense fortune into production before facing the sheer agony of cutting three hundred reels (75 hours) of negatives down to release length of thirteen reels (3½ hours), only to watch audiences walk out on his greatest achievement, shaking their heads in disbelief.

Back on the Fine Arts lot, things were also moving briskly, even without D. W.'s constant attention. As supervising director, Griffith's name was tacked onto the work of Christy Cabanne, John Emerson, Francis J. Grandon, Lloyd Ingraham and Raoul Walsh, all competent directors who were actually responsible for meeting the production requirements of Triangle, and although Griffith found time to look in occasionally, his mind was clearly not on the mundane matters facing Fine Arts production. There were many other windmills with which the artist could joust.

III

A weary Mack Sennett shifted his weight and picked up the silver knife, checking as he always did to make certain it was sharp before attacking the steak before him. Griffith and Ince weren't the only one with problems; he had his share too. Mack's worst fears of working for and with Harry Aitken were being confirmed daily; not even the $1000 weekly salary plus Triangle stock had been sufficient to offset completely his suspicions, especially after making that long trip to La Junta and learning of Harry's plan to secure the services of several name comics from the stage for the proposed Triangle-Keystone Comedies. Coming up the hard way, Mack had taken his share of knocks from the stage and burlesque and he knew that the requirements of the comic stage were not entirely compatible with those of the movie comedy.

A man could be sensational on the stage in front of a live audience, yet lack those particular qualities which the singular eye of the relentlessly staring camera required. A stage act was seen by most of the audience from a considerable distance; fans demanded close-ups of their picture heroes. The art of pantomime for the silent camera was a demanding one, more so than the stage, which allowed verbalization to accompany a routine. While another factor—timing—was a requirement of the stage, the de-

William Collier originally joined Triangle as a comedian with Mack Sennett's Keystone. Here he offers secretary Mae Busch a drink in Wife and Auto Trouble *(Keystone, 1916).*

mands of the movie world were much more exacting—film and time used in shooting retakes were monies wasted. Mack could have gone on and on and on.

Sennett had not been keen about the high salaries paid Aitken's

After a few comic roles which didn't really come off, William Collier (r) moved into dramas like The No-Good Guy *(Ince, 1916), with Enid Markey.*

prized additions to his comic stable; such salaries could not possibly be paid to all his other name comedians. Hard feelings had been the predictable and inevitable result, not only because of the salaries involved, but as much from the fact that these comics had escaped the route all of his other comedians had taken, from lowly Keystone Kop to featured player and then to star, learning and earning as they had developed a following. Even though George Stout instituted a series of weekly salary increases for the Sennett regulars, the Keystone studio manager was unable to bring everyone up to the $2000-a-week level and this, coupled with the obnoxious attitude of some of the stage comics, had immediately caused discord on an otherwise harmonious and efficient lot.

Take Edwin Fitzgerald, for example. As Eddie Foy, he was a big star on the stage, "Seven Little Foys" and all that, yet after signing a year's contract at $1200 weekly, Foy had absolutely refused to "submit himself to the indignities" which Sennett's script writers thought hilarious. In all fairness, thought Sennett, his writers *were* a little on the unusual side—perhaps weird might have been a better word for some of them—but Foy's attitude had been one of plain stubbornness and simple unreasonableness from the beginning. You couldn't allow a comic to dictate what he would or would not do, tying up an entire cast and delaying the production schedule. In a case like that, there was no recourse but to suspend him.

Of course, Mack had to admit, it wasn't all Foy's fault. When he arrived on the lot, Sennett had taken an immediate dislike to him and assigned Ed Frazee to assist Del Henderson in directing the loud-mouthed Irishman. Frazee's experience in directing was extremely limited and Foy resented having an amateur guide his destinies in this new endeavor. And so he had taken to complaining directly to Sennett and the louder he complained, the harder Mack applied the indirect pressure to make him work, resulting in a stalemate. At least, Mack mused, Foy would not cause any more trouble. His suit for back salary during suspension (which he hadn't earned) had been dismissed in court and Eddie was back on the boards.

Rounding out the case against the stage stars, Mack had felt at the time that fans would not necessarily accept them just on the basis of their reputations; they would have to prove themselves. Now it was beginning to appear that once again, he had judged correctly. What to do about Weber and Fields? Fantastic money, their $3500 weekly salary! Had they been worth it at the box-office, Sennett would have been the first to sing their praises, but the earning/cost ratio for his two-reel Triangle-Keystone Comedies had shown a peculiar pattern. Operating as a Triangle producer had increased Sennett's average cost per finished subject about three times above the investment which the profitable two-reel Keystones distributed by Mutual had cost and now the Triangle exhibitors were beginning to express their unhappiness with the new talent. Because of the exclusive distribution to contract clients only, average earnings were held to a few thousand dollars more than the Mutual Keystone had brought in. As he finished the steak, Mack Sennett reflected on the thought that he had much in common with a frustrated squirrel in a treadle cage—both were running faster and not really going anywhere.

But life wasn't really that harsh on Sennett; for an ex-boilermaker with no formal education to speak of, he had done nicely for himself. Most of the studio problems were now filtered through Stout's office, leaving Sennett free of the everyday operation of

Born in Dublin, William Desmond was an ideal choice for the leading role as an Irish newspaper reporter in Paddy O'Hara *(Ince, 1917).*

the lot. For a fellow his age, Stout had a pretty good head on his shoulders and his unquestionable loyalty to Mack's interests made him the only person around Keystone Sennett trusted completely. Of course, every time he approached the boss with a new idea, Sennett automatically said no; if the idea was worthwhile, Stout would have a good case ready to present in its defense and Mack had learned by experience that his business manager never brought up a topic unless he already had figured out its value to Keystone and was ready to defend it vigorously. Invariably, Stout and his ideas were correct.

Things would have looked much brighter to Sennett on this New Year's Day had he not been constantly at war with Mabel Normand. For nine months now, she had given Mack the cold shoulder after discovering him in a compromising position with her friend Mae Busch. While he deeply regretted throwing her downstairs that night, and even more so the broken arm she had suffered as a result of his Irish temper, no amount of apologies or promises had been able to change her mind—their wedding had not taken place and from the way things looked now, it never would.

Mabel had shut her eyes to all of Mack's indiscretions until Mae Busch came along—funny, the girls were still friends even after the fact. Women were a strange lot; these two along with Anne Luther and Teddie Sampson formed "The Dirty Four," a nickname they had given themselves as a result of their concerted use of vulgarity to plague Sennett (who thought a woman should talk like a lady, whether she was or not) when he was in a bad mood. His relations with Mabel had become so strained that within a few days, Sennett was sending her East with Roscoe Arbuckle to make comedies at Fort Lee, New Jersey, but things weren't really as bad as they could have been—Mack still had the Bathing Beauties for comfort and some of them could drive a man right out of his mind. If only he could find a way to do the same to Harry Aitken!

5
For Better—but Worse

HARRY AITKEN NEEDED NO HELP IN CLIMBING WALLS; HE WAS doing very nicely all by himself, for the New Year had brought mixed blessings to "the greatest aggregation of stars ever assembled under one roof." While Aitken's goal had been set at a minimum of 1000 houses as of January 1, 1916, Triangle could claim but 600 signed contracts for its exclusive services. By April 1, the Triangle program would reach its maximum exposure, with 1500 contract clients in the United States. Although the money came in at an annual rate projected in excess of $6.5 million, it somehow disappeared as if the cash register had a bottomless pit instead of a drawer. Some weeks, even the sharpest pencils in the bookkeeping department were hard pressed to balance the books.

Sennett had broken ground for a new $100,000 studio in September 1915. Fire destroyed the Inceville administration building January 11, while Tom Ince was busily engaged in the construction cleanup of his new facilities at Culver City. Having originally secured twelve acres of free land for this ultra-modern plant, the New York Motion Picture Company had discovered with some embarrassment that there really wasn't enough space left to shoot the exterior scenes Ince needed. Rather than continue trekking up to the Santa Monica ranch, Ince had convinced Kessel and Baumann of the wisdom of purchasing an additional 31 acres of land adjoining the Culver City site. Only Griffith was satisfied with his studio space and facilities, and this because he was far too involved in his new project, which would eventually dance across the screen as *Intolerance*. But two new 90-by-180-foot stages and one 70-by-100-foot interior stage had been added to the Fine Arts studio, giving it a total of 130,000 square feet of stage area. All of these capital improvements took cash and while the responsibility for providing them belonged to Kessel and Baumann, much of the financial backing was advanced by Harry Aitken through Triangle. In his inestimable optimism six months before, Harry had seen nothing but good times ahead, providing his juggling act didn't accelerate beyond his ability to control it. Confident that he could carry the organization through its initial rough spots, Aitken had felt the additional new and improved facilities to be necessary, both for their value in expediting production and the favorable public relations such an expansion would inevitably create with the public and exhibitors, who must constantly be reminded that Triangle Plays were the wave of the future. In keeping with the forward-looking image which it had presented, the Triangle offices were moved out of Kessel and Baumann's quarters in the Longacre Building to their plush accommodations in the newly completed Brokaw Building on January 24. The $100,000 annual lease ran for five years and its cost perfectly complemented the Triangle corporate image.

But as 1916 had replaced the old year, troubles began to appear on many fronts. Triangle's Knickerbocker Theatre was shuttered, ostensibly to install a new pipe organ, but in reality, it had played to near-empty houses almost from its opening in September. Something clearly had to be done and quickly; the Triangle showcase theater system was one of the foundations of Aitken's scheme and it had to pay its own way. If not, the anticipated revenue for the year would have to be revised downward while the theater leases remained as fixed operating costs.

Convinced that showmanship was a big part of his theater's difficulty, Harry lured the flamboyant Samuel L. Rothafel away from the Mark Brothers' Strand Theatre to manage the Knickerbocker. He turned the keys over to the pint-sized impresario on Saturday, January 15. When the Knickerbocker reopened with *Peggy,* Hugo Riesenfeld made his motion picture debut directing the orchestra. Aitken was living up to his credo that only the best people available should work for Harry Aitken and if Rothafel wanted Riesenfeld as his orchestra director, he would have him.

Rothafel took one look at the Knickerbocker's books and winced. Here was a theater with a $2.00 minimum admission playing only one show (consisting of 12 to 14 reels) each day. Evaluating the problem, Rothafel quickly concluded that a high rate of seat turnover was necessary to bring the theater out of the red. In order to do this, the potential audience base had to be broadened. Rothafel proposed to institute a policy of continuous showings, reducing each to a maximum of seven reels. He also prescribed vaudeville acts between the shows and a slashing of admissions to twenty-five cents and fifty cents per seat, holding only a few at the $2.00 price to fulfill the terms of Triangle's lease. When Rothafel made these recommendations to his new employer, Harry did not try to hide his disappointment over the failure of his movie palace concept, but quickly embraced the prescription. Swallowing this bitter medicine, he gave his new manager a pat on the back and instructions to implement the program as he saw fit. His single admonishment to Rothafel was simply, "Turn a profit."

But when the Goelet estate administrators learned of this move, they exploded, along with Robert W. Goelet, heir to the estate. As owner of the Knickerbocker, the estate had leased it to Klaw and Erlanger and the Charles Frohman Company for use as a legitimate stage theater; Triangle's occupancy was by virtue of a sublease. An application for an injunction was filed against the principals of the lease and sublease on February 1, seeking to enjoin Triangle from presenting continuous motion pictures with singers, vaudeville acts and an orchestra in support. As the plaintiff, Robert Goelet contended that the sale of orchestra seats at the reduced admission price was in clear violation of the terms of the original lease and injurious to both the reputation and classification of his deceased father's theatre.

Not really a serious matter to the casual observer, the request for an injunction would prove to be one of those minor annoyances which often precede utter catastrophe. Within six weeks after the suit had been filed, Triangle's right to use the theatre structure in the more conventional way had been strongly reaffirmed by an opinion[1] handed down by Justice Daniel F. Cohalan of the New York State Supreme Court. Presented with little more than a series of affidavits from prominent citizens which supported Goelet's contention that Rothafel's managerial policy was injurious to the theatre's potential value, Justice Cohalan held that Triangle had not in fact actually violated the terms of either the original lease or its sublease, although agreeing in principle with Goelet's contention that the new policy might hurt the theatre's name, a point he made clear in his opinion.

---

[1] *Goelet v. Frohman, Inc., et al., New York Law Journal,* February 23, 1916, p. 1902.

William Desmond's forte was rugged action and Lieutenant Danny of the U.S.A. *(Ince, 1916) gave him one of his best Triangle roles. Written around the contemporary Mexican border troubles, it co-starred Enid Markey as a south-of-the-border señorita.*

"Through the introduction of moving pictures and photoplays into the theatrical field, there has occurred therein an evolution in the production and presentation of plays. In fact, the entire trend of the business may have so evolved as to permit the defendants to carry on their business as now being conducted without violating the restrictive covenants of the lease. Even though irreparable injury may be shown in view of the short time the lease has to run, unless the right of those seeking the injunction is clear and unmistakable, this court may not intervene to prevent the use of the theatre in the manner that it is now being conducted."

As a result, Goelet had no choice but to relent, but a few months later, he managed to have the last laugh—on August 22, another suit was entered in the State Supreme Court against Harry Aitken. This time, it was his lessors, Charles Frohman Inc., Al Hayman, Marc Klaw and A. L. Erlanger, who instituted the action in an effort to collect the $5000 back rent owed by Triangle on its Knickerbocker lease. The entire affair came to a close with a rather sad ending for the old theater which had once been anointed with stardust as Harry Aitken had set forth to exploit his glorious dream. It was again sublet but on April 29, 1917, the Knickerbocker closed its doors once more; this time for another remodeling before returning to legitimate stage productions that fall.

Unfortunately for Triangle, its abortive attempt to establish a series of motion picture palaces in major cities across the nation was not the only illness to afflict Aitken's master plan. When Triangle opened its doors for business, Harry had quite reasonably expected a prompt, favorable response from both exhibitors and the public and his expectations had come true; in great demand, Triangle Plays were reasonably popular at the outset but this blissful state of affairs lasted only a few short weeks. As 1915 passed into 1916, a considerable number of the Triangle contract clients, who were paying rentals quite in excess of the usual fees, had become increasingly disenchanted with their supplier. Pictures announced for release were quite often replaced with substitutes at the last moment, a fault which rested more with the confused New York office, where titles were scheduled and rescheduled with the ease of shuffling a deck of cards, than with its production facilities.

Although Aitken had been sincere in his enthusiasm for the future of the motion picture, and especially his Triangle Plays, Harry had made his first major misjudgment in a career which had been studded with successes, some genuine and some just plain luck. During 1916, he would compound that error with disastrous results. It was now clearly evident to all that the stage star experi-

While most of William Desmond's Triangle Plays were action dramas, he occasionally turned up in melodramatic sob stories like Sorrows of Love *(Ince, 1916), with Bessie Barriscale. Its cost—$18,859.23.*

ment was failing and failing badly. The silent drama would not replace the spoken stage, at least not at this time. When Harry had conceived the idea of Triangle, he had never once doubted its commercial success, believing that it would follow much the same path as had *The Birth of a Nation*. His unusual imagination and business acumen had anticipated the majority of sequential events that were to follow the founding of Triangle, and as a result, he had been prepared to meet them. His understanding of production, promotion, corporate structure, organization and finance had attracted the attention and support of respected Wall Street bankers and Aitken had taken care to sign the best production talents in the business.

But Harry had failed to correctly estimate two major factors—his player roster and the audiences—the two keys to whatever degree of success Triangle was ever to enjoy. His stage actors, accustomed to earning $200 to $500 weekly for 26 to 39 weeks (when their plays were successful) had been so afraid of the effects of screen appearances on their stage reputations that Arthur Klein had been forced to offer double and even quadruple salaries on a firm one-year contract basis to convince them to make the move. At this same time, the experienced screen actors who had acquired a following at the box-office were being paid $100 to $300 weekly and were very unhappy over the acquisition of their legitimate stage competition at the higher rates. This unhealthy state of affairs was further complicated when it was discovered that many of the stage actors required take after take before the camera could capture just the right effect; others were not really

William Desmond was one of the few stage stars brought to the screen in 1915 by Triangle who carved a lengthy career from the magic lantern beams; in the twenties, Bill was Universal's leading serial hero. Here he lends a hand to a charity drive.

photogenic and the camera blatantly emphasized their flaws for all to see in closeup after closeup. The competition between the stage stars and movie actors soon became the source of bitter tension on-set, especially since many of the former were content simply to ride out their contracts, collect their inflated wages and return to the stage that much richer.

In just a few months, the theatrical actors managed by default to convince their less-prosperous co-workers that there was very little to fear from their presence on the lot, a fact soon endorsed by movie fans across the nation. Exhibitors had started to scream that the fabulous stars of Broadway were even more fabulous failures on their screens. Audiences deserted the theaters which ran Triangle Plays and as a result, exhibitors began to rebel against the high rentals necessitated by the increased production costs, which reflected the high salaries of the stage stars and their unfamiliarity with camera techniques. At a time when his production schedule was straining from the burden of expenses far greater than those of his competitors, Harry was faced with the prospect of an avalanche of cancelled contracts. News of this state of affairs brought the acquisition of new theater contracts to a virtual halt, as developments of this kind travelled rapidly along the exhibitors' pipelines. Thus, the market for Triangle product began to shrink slowly but with an ominous regularity, and amazingly enough this had all taken place in just six months.

It had all seemed so simple—Harry's theory had gone something like this: *The Birth of a Nation* was grossing millions and while no intelligent person would realistically assume that the Triangle program pictures would repeat this financial windfall to the penny, it did seem a logical premise that each could be expected to gross up to a million dollars. Give the public sophisticated entertainment, it would respond and exhibitors would knock down Triangle's doors trying to get in on a good thing. The more theaters under Triangle's wing, the greater the gross earnings and resulting profits. All very reasonable in an industry where the average earnings of a feature picture were between $50,000 and $100,000.

But what Aitken had failed to take into account was the nature of the audience—those who constituted the bulk of potential paying patrons in 1915-16 were not interested in sophisticated entertainment; many were from that economic group we would call deprived by today's terms. Still the domain of the immigrant and working class, the motion picture theater had not been taken over by the middle class at that time. While many today still recall the delight of subtitles and credit them with improving their reading ability, the truth of the matter was that subtitles and lengthy summations of plots on the screen using the written word interfered with the enjoyment of the typical patron. To have succeeded as Harry had planned, Triangle Plays would have needed the support of the middle class and the intellectuals, and neither were ready or willing to give that support in the form of cash.

The industry's average cost range of a program picture was in the neighborhood of $10,000 to $30,000. Add to that another $10,000 for release prints and advertising, and the film went to theater circuits costing its producer somewhere between $20,000 and $40,000. After distribution fees and his investment had been returned, the average net profit to the producer hovered in the area of $10,000 to $20,000, to which another like sum could be added for foreign sales. On an annual basis, it was entirely possible to earn a net profit of between one and two million dollars from a program of feature film production—Adolph Zukor did it. But the system choked if the per picture overhead climbed only a few thousand dollars—profits were wiped out, and this was substantially Triangle's problem. The anticipated gross did not materialize and an exchange system which cost in excess of one-half million dollars per year to operate failed to earn its keep. Although the public was led to believe that Triangle invested $50,000 to $200,000 in each film, its cost per picture (an average $20,000) was considerably below that range, but more than double the production costs of the competition.[2] Had Triangle actually invested what it claimed in each picture, the corporation would have been in a receiver's hands within three to four months after beginning business. As it was, bankruptcy would take a bit longer and a helping hand in the till.

When the fiscal pinch began to make itself felt, Triangle reached into the vault, pulling out several of the features previously made for Mutual distribution, but not used in fulfilling contract requirements. *D'Artagnan* was one such picture sold to the public as a super-special. Put in the can by Tom Ince for $17,774, its cost was somewhat higher than that of his other productions of 1914-15, but just slightly under the cost of his 1916 operation. Ince's Tri-

---

[2] By 1917, the situation would be reversed—Triangle pictures came in at $15,000 to $25,000 while its leading competitors were spending four times that sum.

When Bill Desmond was not swashbuckling through action epics for Triangle, he spent his time in society dramas, usually with Bessie Barriscale as his leading lady. This scene (minus Desmond) came from their Not My Sister (Ince, 1916), with Monte Blue doing the explaining to a distraught Bessie. Standing beside her is a young Alice Terry, who would hit stardom five years later with Valentino in The Four Horsemen of the Apocalypse.

One-time Ince favorites Rhea Mitchell and Orrin Johnson remained at Triangle after their mentor had departed, appearing in dramatic nonsense like Whither Thou Goest (Triangle Foursquare, 1918). Both careers were now on the wane.

Pretty Pauline Starke made a series of action-packed melodramas for the near-defunct Triangle in 1918, often working with Roy Stewart, holding bottle in this scene from Irish Eyes.

By 1919, star value in Triangle Plays had disappeared. Leads were carried by such venerable character actors as Wilbur Higby, J. Barney Sherry and Jack Richardson, seen here in The Mayor of Filbert.

angle Pictures averaged $19,444 to produce. It wasn't a particularly exciting picture but did remain fairly faithful to the Dumas story and fitted in rather nicely with the rest of the slow-moving Triangle program. As Triangle had already bought this group of pictures from the production companies, their use helped to balance an otherwise bleak financial sheet during the year.

By April 1916, theater patronage at Triangle Plays had dropped off so sharply that the Triangle publicity department attempted a sharp departure from its policy in *The Triangle,* a publication made available to contracting exhibitors. Switching from the soft sell to the hard push, Triangle began exhorting its exhibitors to deliver an eight-point, 15 minute lecture between showings, ostensibly to "bring to the consciousness of the patronage those aims and ideals of the producers of Triangle plays, and the work involved in making them." Illustrated with sixteen lantern slides provided by the Triangle exchanges, this was a desperate attempt to appeal to the audiences for their continued support. The publicity department suggested the following eight points should be stressed:

(1) How Triangle pictures were made.
(2) What Triangle pictures cost to produce.
(3) The energy and mentality behind the Triangle Plays.
(4) Why theaters using Triangle pictures paid more for them.
(5) Why the public paid more to see Triangle pictures.
(6) How the public's nickels, dimes and quarters influenced the work of Triangle producers.
(7) How the public's support affected theater programs.
(8) An appeal to the public spirit of the theatergoer to shoulder the responsibility for the class of entertainment shown in his neighborhood.

Quite a serving for one 15 minute lecture! A presentation of this nature was an appeal to the intellectuals and critics who had loudly acclaimed the aims and ideals of Triangle when it was formed, but who had been the first to drop out. In theater after theater where this bold-faced plea was attempted, audiences did not bother to wait for the picture to bore them; they got up and left in the middle of the sermon.

Almost from the beginning, exhibitors tied to the Triangle way began to chafe under the restrictions which prevented their use of other films. Had they been allowed to present other producers' pictures along with their Triangle Plays, that might have proven the prop necessary to hold up the Triangle program and buy the time Harry Aitken needed to seek a resolution of his unforeseen problems.[3] But this was not to be the case; Triangle remained adamant in its avowal that Triangle Plays should, could and would stand alone, even when advised otherwise by its own vice-presidents; Griffith, Ince and Sennett favored unrestricted distribution of Triangle product to any and all theaters wishing to use it, regardless of contract (and they stood accused of wishing only to fatten their own purses) or Harry Aitken.

As its cost/earning ratio became more and more disproportionate, Triangle acquired the singularly unpopular habit of requiring larger and larger deposits paid to its exchanges well in advance of film delivery. No exhibitor who had managed to survive in the bitterly competitive arena of the motion picture jungle was blind enough to be convinced otherwise for one moment—Triangle was starting to finance its production schedule with their money, an incredible state of affairs. Was not Triangle the colossus of the motion picture world, with the unlimited financial backing of Wall Street and the greatest talent in the business producing for it?

True enough, Triangle had placed its stock on the curb market shortly after its formation in July 1915 at a price of $5.00 per share.[4] Public acceptance of the concept behind Triangle and the names of Griffith, Ince and Sennett as associates had sent the price up to $7.00 almost immediately. On August 30, the stock had stood at 6-7/8 and after the successful opening at the Knickerbocker a month later, moved up to 8¾. But October saw it drop back to 7, wavering in the 7-6 range through early 1916 while investors and the market watched to see what Harry Aitken could and would do. Well aware by then that Triangle's assets were highly overvalued in relation to their earnings, Harry's financial backers were no longer willing to commit their funds beyond what had already been extended and instituted a freeze on additional capital. By September 30, 1916, Triangle's basic flaws could no longer be hidden, no more stock could be issued and the price

---

[3] Looking at the other side of the coin, it is just as logical to believe that Aitken realized exhibitors might well have abandoned the Triangle product completely had they been given this option.

[4] Triangle was the second motion picture corporation to go public. World Film Corporation under Arthur Spiegel had preceded it on the curb market, now known as the over-the-counter market.

H. O. Davis nearly rescued Triangle from its desperate plight during 1917–18, despite Harry Aitken. Instituting a cost effectiveness program, he pared many of the non-essentials from Triangle's operation and although many considered him a creative catastrophe, he produced profitable low-budget pictures which gave Triangle a second lease on life.

of the outstanding shares ($2.00) reflected the market's growing lack of faith in the wizardry of Triangle's corporate management and policies. The day of reckoning was fast approaching and no amount of hustling on Harry's part seemed to slow it down perceptibly.

6

Rascals of Wolfish Ways

AS EXECUTIVE HEADS OF THEIR NEW YORK MOTION PICTURE COMpany, Adam Kessel and Charlie Baumann could not have been more incongruous. Kessel, a former publisher of *The Sporting Gazette,* was a thin, wiry ex-gambler who had fallen into the motion picture exchange business quite by accident while collecting a debt and, recognizing its great potential after a few weeks of operation, soon brought his good friend and one-time racetrack tout Baumann into the fold to share the good fortune with him. Charlie, a short, stocky man with a swarthy complexion, cheerfully admitted to once having been a trolley car conductor whose path to success had been paved by withholding countless fares from his employers, a fact of which he was not only proud, but one that formed the basis of his favorite story, which he never tired of telling, much to the embarrassment of his close associates.

Shrewd operators who had found a golden goose, these two men had severed their active participation in the business end of gambling, as a result of new state legislation governing race tracks in New York, but both retained a fondness for the art. In an effort to secure new and different films for their Empire Exchanges, Kessel and Baumann combined forces with producer Fred Balshofer and lawyer Louis Burstein in 1909 to open the New York Motion Picture Company, entering the production arena under the banner of their newly formed Bison Films. With Balshofer directing and Arthur Miller behind the camera, their early pictures were successful enough to draw the attention of the Motion Picture Patents Company and it was touch and go for a couple of years with filming moving from the Fort Lee, New Jersey, area to the Catskill Mountains of New York and finally out West, always

William Christy Cabanne, Griffith's "chief of staff" at Triangle, spent five years with "The Master" and directed many of the Griffith-supervised Fine Arts productions. Upset with Triangle's policies, he was finally lured away in late 1916 by Louis B. Mayer to direct Francis X. Bushman's only serial, The Great Secret.

just a half-step ahead of prosecution by the Trust. But the wave of the cinema's future rested with those independents who dared challenge the monopoly of the Patents Company and by 1912, Kessel and Baumann's business had become a reasonably settled and very prosperous affair, thanks to the popular films produced by Tom Ince.

New York's old Polo Grounds was their second home thereafter; their corporate working day seemed to average about two hours daily. The boys would hurriedly rush into their large office in the Longacre Building in the morning, just in time to order an early lunch sent up from a nearby restaurant. The usual format of their short working day included the signing of letters, dictating replies to the correspondence which their secretary had prepared for their arrival and arguing over which team would win the afternoon's ball game before leaving for the ball park. May Kenny, an unusually loyal and efficient secretary, ran the office in their absence and she earned every penny of the $75.00 paid her each week, in an era when the average secretary drew $20.00. During their troubles with Universal in 1912, it had been Miss Kenny who tipped the two off to an impending raid on their offices by the Universal forces and Kessel and Baumann never forgot her help in those trying moments.

Harry Aitken in 1916, surrounded by a group of his Triangle stars. BOTTOM: *Douglas Fairbanks, Bessie Love, Constance Talmadge, Constance Collier, Lillian Gish, Fay Tincher, De Wolf Hopper.* CENTER: *Robert Harron, Aitken, Sir Herbert Beerbohm Tree, Owen Moore, Wilfred Lucas.* TOP: *Dorothy Gish, Seena Owen, Norma Talmadge.*

But the reader should not get the impression that Kessel and Baumann had a business which ran itself completely for them, or that Miss Kenny was actually the brains behind it, or even that the boys were the pair of clowns Mack Sennett made them out to be in his autobiography, *King of Comedy*. It should merely be noted that by 1915, they had a smoothly functioning business operating on the product furnished by Sennett and Ince on the West Coast (both moneymakers in their own right) and as long as no one tipped the ship of state, all ran fairly quietly. Once they connected with Harry Aitken, Kessel and Baumann had someone to bail them out of whatever bad luck might befall them, and increasingly they prevailed upon his good offices. If the boys were hard pressed for money (usually as a result of heavy gambling losses), Aitken stood out as a rock in the storm to bolster their operation and he did so more than once. He actually had no choice; their product was the mainstay of the Triangle release schedule and they constantly wielded this fact as a club over Harry's head.

Both men loved the good living, prestige and working hours associated with their New York Motion Picture Company, and while neither tried very hard to disguise his lower-class Brooklyn upbringing, each was clever enough and sufficiently well versed in the realities of the everyday world to realize that while a certain degree of irresponsibility was acceptable and even desirable, there was a point beyond which it could not be tolerated. In short, they were happy-go-lucky to a degree, but as tough as necessary when the situation demanded it (and sometimes when it didn't). The relationship between Ad and Charlie was a stormy one and often found them at cross-purposes, mediated only by their attorney who attended each board meeting for a retainer of $250. His function was not to tell them what they *could* do, but to guard against their embarking upon some course of action which was *not legal*. Board meetings were the essence of informality, with their legal eagle casually occupying the overstuffed leather sofa in a comfortable prone position, sitting upright only to say no whenever he found it appropriate, which was quite often.

It was this attitude of always seeking an "angle," coupled with a complete but covert disavowal of loyalty to Triangle (except for drawing their $900 pay check each week) and a bank balance that never seemed to remain above the point of solvency for long, which plagued Harry to the point that the three men were often

Adam Kessel, circa 1913. While pictures of Harry Aitken are relatively abundant, those of Ad Kessel and Charlie Baumann are extremely difficult to locate. The author has only seen a handful of pictures of these two. A stylish dresser, Kessel didn't look like an ex-racetrack tout, but his contemporaries in the business remember him as exuding the air of sharpness associated with the stereotype "turn-of-the-century" bookie, while playing straight man for Baumann. It is not unfair to say that while Kessel was the business head of the New York Motion Picture Company, Baumann was the joie de vivre.

seen fighting each other in a comic atmosphere reminiscent of the best of Gilbert and Sullivan. Interestingly enough, for all of their other shortcomings, the boys were never mixed up with the developing sabotage of Triangle's financial position and when they eventually discovered what had happened to the corporate treasury, were absolutely speechless for days, not so much because it had been done, but because it had been accomplished right under their own noses and not only were they unaware of it, they hadn't been invited to participate.

Kessel and Baumann's periodic trips to the West Coast were primarily vacation excursions, even when there was work to be done. Once there, they attempted to act the part of managers and George W. Stout, the Keystone studio manager, still chuckles over the day Adam Kessel called him over to a dismantled set and inquired why none of the bent nails lying around had been collected, straightened and used over. Stout's explanation that the labor costs

Griffith's memorable epic, The Birth of a Nation, *made the Triangle Film Corporation possible by its outstanding performance at the box-office, bearing out Harry Aitken's contention that there was a market for the $2.00 picture. It should be noted that $2.00 was the top price for a seat, not the general admission. Originally released on the state-right market by Epoch Producing Corporation, the film was also distributed under the auspices of Triangle, as this main title frame shows. The financing and copyright complications surrounding* The Birth of a Nation *have been as confused and bitter over the years as the violent reactions it has brought from audiences.*

to do so would be excessive and that the carpenters would refuse to use a straightened nail anyway went completely over Ad's head, failing to make any impression whatsoever. Kessel's verdict was immediate—Stout wasn't managing the lot as cheaply and efficiently as he might. When informed of Stout's lack of cost-consciousness, Sennett wisely thanked his partner, promising to take the matter up with the studio manager at the first opportunity, a complaint he never voiced a word about to Stout. This incident amusingly took place at a time when Kessel and Baumann were continually echoing

Mae Marsh differed from the usual Griffith heroine, lacking the delicate, ethereal qualities of Lillian Gish and Mary Pickford. But Mae was a fine actress and made an interesting series of "little" films with Bobby Harron (l) while at Triangle. This scene is from The Wharf Rat *(Fine Arts, 1916), with Spottiswoode Aitken (r).*

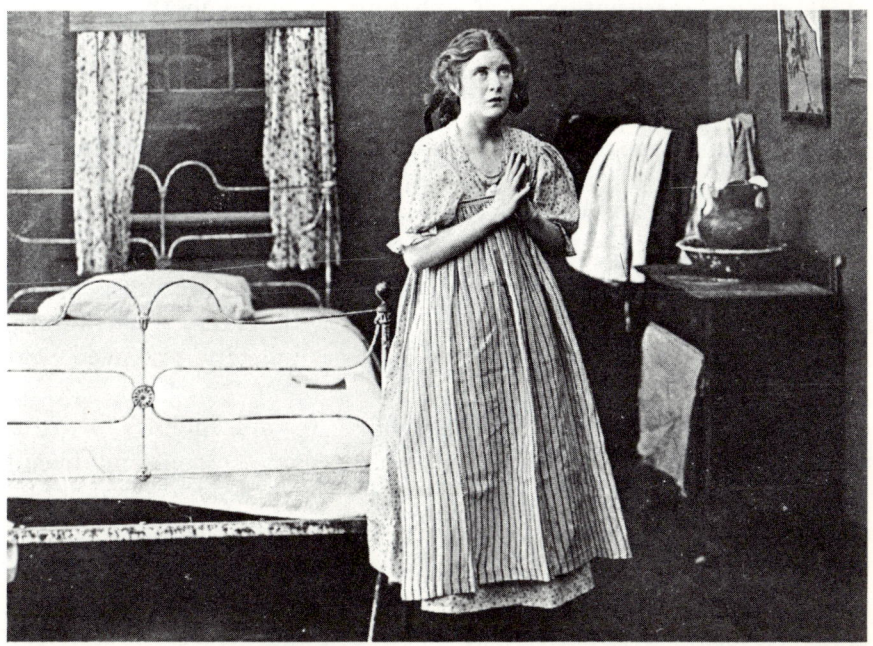

Usually cast as the adolescent who was thrust into womanhood by the situations she encountered, Mae Marsh gave many fine performances for Griffith. Joining her older sister Marguerite on the screen in 1910, Mae enjoyed a long career which saw her named as one of the five best actresses of the silent era in a George Eastman House award of 1955. Soon after A Little Liar *(Fine Arts, 1916) was released, she joined Goldwyn but interestingly enough, her one good role in the twenties came in* The White Rose *(1923), a reunion with D. W. Griffith.*

Harry Aitken's slogan in telegram after telegram to their West Coast producers—"Spend more money!"

Toward the end of his association with Triangle, Kessel bought a summer home near Keeseville, New York, and developed a fondness for cruising up Lake Champlain in the summer. He had suffered what was termed a nervous breakdown in December 1916 just after his fiftieth birthday and recovered very slowly, spending as much of 1917 as possible out of the office. This state of affairs didn't bother Harry Aitken at all, for by this time, he had no taste left for repeated encounters with Kessel. There were too many other affairs which needed his attention without constantly banging heads with Ad.

Harry Aitken had certainly come a long way from his middle-class childhood in Waukesha, Wisconsin. It had been a long, eventful but profitable haul and he was now the unchallenged head of a multi-million dollar corporation, with a life style which reflected his position in a relaxed, casual manner. Harry did not have to work hard at living a life of comparative financial ease, as did his partners; it came to him naturally. The best clothes, the best of foods and association with uplifting company in the form of captains of industry and finance—that was life as he saw it and Harry was determined to make the best of it.

His luxurious seven-room apartment in the West Fifties was located near Carnegie Hall and housed both his butler and maid (who also provided the services of a cook). It was elegant, yet simple and reflected taste—not necessarily all Harry's. His secretary, Miss Harrison, often doubled as Harry's interior decorator in addition to her other duties. Aitken entertained extensively on a selective basis and an invitation to sup with Harry at his apartment always meant the finest in food, exquisitely prepared and properly served.

Harry's taste for the best extended to automobiles also; a nearby basement garage housed his chauffeur, a long-time friend from childhood days back in Waukesha who now made himself available on a 24-hour basis to drive Aitken whenever or wherever his whims or business affairs might take him. As chauffeur, he was in charge of Harry's four cars—a Mercedes, Fiat and two Rolls Royces; no American automobile manufacturer offered the opulence Aitken demanded.

Harry was one of those rare individuals able to organize himself to maximize the value of time almost unconsciously. The clock meant nothing to him and he was likely to put in 24 hours consecutively without once thinking of sleep. Miss Harrison had her desk right outside Harry's office and she complemented the Aitken working pattern—extreme efficiency. When it came time for him to take a cross-country trip to visit the studios, all that he needed was to mention the dates he would be out of town and she arranged the rest. On the day of his departure, the tickets for his drawing room were handed to him, usually with a minimum of $1500 from company funds for pocket money; Harry never liked to be caught short. If his trip was an extended one, the butler and maid would be on board the train when it left New York, as well as the chauffeur, who would find Harry's fifth car (another Rolls Royce permanently stored in Los Angeles for just such an occasion) awaiting him at the station, ready to take the entire party to the Beverly Hills Hotel, where a suite had been reserved. All this was courtesy of Miss Harrison's arrangements, for she saw to it that her employer had as few mundane matters as possible to occupy his mind and time.

Harry Aitken wore the good life easily, just as some men appear to be nattily dressed even in rags. No one who had occasion to work around him would have guessed his humble beginnings. But Harry was a man driven by an inner compulsion—he had to have the best, work the hardest, think up the most novel schemes—and it was this drive which in the end would burn his candle out thirty years before his death. He firmly believed that success bred success and although he admitted that failure was always a possibility, Harry considered it a remote circumstance. Think big and everything would come true, provided that the thoughts were accompanied by hard work. It almost seemed as if he sometimes wore blinders to avoid distractions as he forged ahead.

And for awhile, it looked as if the Aitken philosophy of positive thinking was indeed a foolproof formula for success; from the operation of a nickelodeon to an independent exchange to president of Mutual and now Triangle—how much further could Harry Aitken go? The sky was the limit in his mind, but Harry had no conception of how close he really was to that sky, or that its ceiling was lowering each day.

During 1916, he would gradually change, so gradually that even he himself would not notice the alteration. But desperation has a way of multiplying itself and Harry was slowly becoming a desperate man. He became edgy and nervous, prone to worrying and

Acknowledged by all for decades as the finest director during the formative years of the motion picture, D. W. Griffith was at the height of his fame and creativity during 1915–16, when he placed both The Birth of a Nation *and* Intolerance *on the screen. His legend is now under reevaluation by cinema historians and critics, whose temptation to rewrite the past is almost too great to forego. While still acknowledging his contributions, the trend is to downplay positive considerations and emphasize his failings. The definitive biography of "The Master" has yet to appear, although his long-time friend and author Seymour Stern has been at work for years collecting and evaluating Griffith minutiae.*

sometimes hesitant to move for no apparent reason. The toll of Triangle was beginning to catch up with the gregarious promoter and internal squabbles with Kessel and Baumann, his financial

Seena Owen's screen career began with a chance meeting of an old friend, director Marshall Neilan. Neilan sent her to D. W. Griffith, who thought her appearance and personality too cold for the screen, but hired her anyway.

backers and three producers steadily increased. The pressure of a business which failed to catch fire combined with a variety of solutions that failed to provide the relief necessary. Yet Harry held fast to his original concept of Triangle and the harder Ince and Sennett pressed him to make what they felt to be desirable and necessary changes in organizational procedure, the more firmly he resisted their advice. As a result, Harry had no one to blame but himself—he had sown the seeds of his own disaster with the foundation of Triangle—and he would soon reap the bitter harvest.

7

The Cure that Failed

TRIANGLE'S FINANCIAL POSITION IN EARLY 1916 WAS BECOMING more and more precarious each week. Its pictures were limited in distribution to contracting theaters, the number of which had fallen far short of Harry's original expectations. For some unexplainable reason, Aitken refused to accept the fact that the very exclusiveness of the Triangle Plays remained the major stumbling block to their increased distribution, which would have greatly enhanced their competitive chances at the box-office. Instead, he chose to pursue what he felt was the one avenue of escape for Harry Aitken and Triangle; a merger of facilities and assets with another production company, one that possessed the basic strengths lacking in Triangle. Such an arrangement and its resulting vast conglomerate appealed to Harry's vanity; it would have allowed him to retain his position of prominence in the industry while providing both the time and capital to realign the Triangle program concept closer to what movie audiences and exhibitors wanted. And it just so happened that at this time when it was needed most, a reasonable possibility for infusing new life into the dying organization appeared in the person of one Benjamin B. Hampton.

In his capacity as a vice-president of the American Tobacco Company, Hampton had been concerned for some time over how to most profitably invest a $100 million surplus of American Tobacco capital. After undertaking a careful investigation of possible investment alternatives, which occupied much of his time during 1915, Hampton had decided that the motion picture industry offered investors a fantastic growth potential. While his study had encompassed both the personnel and corporate structures of the more than 200 active production and/or distribution companies in

102

Seena Owen as "The Princess Beloved" in the Babylonian episode of Intolerance *(Griffith, 1916).*

existence during 1915, it was the birth of Triangle which he had watched with special interest. From the resulting mass of data and information gathered, Hampton had concluded that a corporation capitalized at between fifteen and twenty million dollars could be financed in Wall Street and sold to investors. And just as he had arrived at his conclusions, along came Harry Aitken to do that very same thing, only on a somewhat smaller scale.

Initially favoring a combination of Paramount interests and V L S E,[1] Hampton had won approval from his management to go ahead and see what could be done to bring these two organizations together, using American Tobacco's surplus capital. This assignment proved to be an eye-opening experience for the business executive, who soon discovered that motion pictures had bred a different kind of executive than he had ever before encountered. Proud, vain and jealous, these semi-illiterate men had stumbled into positions of great wealth and power, partially by being in the right place at the right time, but also because of their primitive entrepreneuring nature and a great desire to improve their positions in life. Possession of a common affinity with the tastes of those to whom the motion picture appealed had allowed them to recognize the medium's inherent entertainment potential long before men like Hampton discovered it.[2]

Paramount was a distribution organization founded in 1915 by William Wadsworth Hodkinson to handle the product of Adolph Zukor's Famous Players and Jesse Lasky's Feature Film Company on a 25-year exclusive distribution contract. V S L E was the dying gasp of four production firms which had recognized that the great days of the Motion Picture Patents Company, along with its releasing arm, General Film, were over.[3] Although continuing to release short subjects through General Film, they had at the same time stepped outside the Trust to produce and release five-reel features in an effort to keep solvent by competing in the growing market for longer pictures.

A merger of the sort Hampton had in mind required that at least seven executive chains of command he reduced to one and therein the naive outsider met with a solid wall of resistance. All kinds of small empires, some stagnant, some still growing, had been carefully constructed and cultivated within these chains of

[1] Vitagraph, Lubin, Selig and Essanay.

[2] Although often portrayed as uneducated and poor, many of the pioneer producers had carved comfortable financial careers for themselves before turning to the movies. Zukor, Mayer, Fox, Laemmle were among the group whose primary concern was as much respectability as it was money; while the fur, clothing and junk businesses were profitable for these immigrants, the sight of the city's leading junk merchant walking down the streets was not likely to make much of an impression on those with social prestige, and it was power and prestige as much as money which drew these men into the speculation of motion pictures.

[3] While Vitagraph had recently discharged over two dozen actors, Lubin was far behind on his payments to banks holding his notes; Selig was thought of as a pro-German sympathizer in a day when public opinion was swinging to England and France, and Essanay's pictures were simply and undeniably bad.

While spectacles may come and go, high costs have closed the door forever on magnificent sets such as these from D. W. Griffith's Intolerance (1916). *A critical success but box-office failure when originally released, it's not stretching the truth too much to say that* Intolerance *has created more interest in the past decade than it did at its debut over a half-century ago.*

command by the executives concerned. With an eye toward his money, all gave verbal assurances of favoring Hampton's proposal, but each saw himself as the dominant figure in any new conglomeration to be arrived at and none wished to be eased out of a plush job. Hampton's proposal called for representatives of both the Zukor and Lasky groups to be taken into the new corporation as stockholders; they would not join under any other circumstances. Hodkinson was adamant in his refusal to allow this to happen, partially from a streak of stubbornness, but to a larger degree from a fear of being swallowed alive by Zukor and Lasky, who had exhibited alarming ambitions over the past few months. Such turbulent feelings could not help but sink the tobacco ship with its cargo of operating capital and negotiations came to a halt.

Enter Harry Aitken, who had gone West on February 17 under the guise of an inspection tour of his production facilities but

106 *Dreams For Sale*

Accused by his critics in the twenties of having lost touch with the realities of the cinema, D. W. Griffith fought back with pictures like Orphans of the Storm, The White Rose *and* America, *but to no avail. His unforgiveable sin had been the box-office failure of* Intolerance *(1916), which cost him his fortune and creative control over his own destiny. Rejected in later years by the industry he helped create, Griffith looked back on a past filled with cinematic triumphs and failures contained in the collage of production stills mounted over the mantle in the scene above, representing some of the American motion picture's greatest moments.*

Thirty-five years old when the Triangle Film Corporation was founded, the youthful Mack Sennett had already created the basis for a legend with his extremely popular Keystone Comedies, which became a mainstay of the Triangle program. Kops and custard pies were central to the legend, which would soon emerge in all its press-agented splendor with the acclamation of Sennett as "The King of Comedy."

with the primary purpose of determining what chance Triangle stood to be included in this huge largess. Contacting Hampton, Harry indicated his willingness to count his corporation in and Triangle's name, as well as that of Mutual, went into the rumor mill as another possible partner for Hampton's planned merger.[4] But unfortunately for Harry and Triangle, Hampton was already well aware of the multitude of problems facing the continued existence of this too-willing would-be partner and Aitken found himself sitting in a card game with little more than the names of his three producers with which to bid, a rather slender and somewhat depressing hand that couldn't stand scrutiny after the opening bid. His 22-unit exchange system was a virtual duplicate of those owned by other major production films; and although the Triangle player roster was a formidable one on paper, in reality it was top heavy with high-priced failures.

After failing in his effort to make a definite connection with Hampton, Harry sought out Jesse Lasky and Samuel Goldfish, with whom he began to spend a good deal of time. This move was made against the better judgment of his brother Roy, who recognized that Harry was greatly outclassed in the art of machination. But Harry was desperately trying to get a piece of the action for Triangle and to do so he would deal with anyone, even Adolph Zukor, an innately shrewd and self-made executive whose formal education bore no relationship to his actual talent or achievements. Zukor had picked Hampton's brain of whatever data was necessary and helpful before turning him down and putting the information to work in a concerted drive for dominance in the industry. With his Wall Street connections, Aitken was also in a position to serve a useful purpose and so Zukor assiduously courted Harry, dangling the prospects of a merger between their two organizations. The precise motivation for this courtship is unknown, but in view of what took place only a short time after, it is quite reasonable to suspect Zukor of using Aitken, gaining sufficient information to allow him to analyze Triangle's methods of finance, organizational strengths and weaknesses and thus to determine the true value of its various properties. Although he realized the precarious position in which he was placing Triangle, Harry could see no alternative but to open the books for the little Hungarian to pore over as he

---

[4] John R. Freuler had still not arrived at the inescapable conclusion that he didn't have whatever it took to operate a multimillion dollar corporation successfully—and Mutual had continued to steadily lose ground under his directorship.

had asked, trusting to a faint glimmer of humanity that Zukor was truly sincere in the discussions. This move allowed Aitken's competitors to freely develop an accurate picture of his competitive position.

In the meantime, Benjamin Hampton had made his decision. One million dollars of American Tobacco money went to Vitagraph, allowing the firm to absorb the entire V L S E operation and reorganize as Greater Vitagraph. The corporation which had begun business just before the turn of the century with a capitalization of $6000 was now recapitalized in 1916 for $25,000,000. For his contribution, Hampton was given four seats on the board of directors and he promptly selected Frank H. Hitchcock, H. H. Vreeland and Clendenin J. Ryan to accompany him into the exalted atmosphere of the motion picture business.[5]

A few weeks before, J. Stuart Blackton, who had shared Vitagraph's ownership with Albert E. Smith and William T. Rock from its very beginning, had spoken to the press on the rumored involvement of Vitagraph with American Tobacco, commenting at the time, "A state of overproduction, at a ratio of 5 to 1, exists in the business. This is bound to bring about a readjustment. I have no doubt that it is about here and that the many rumors arise from that fact..... for the good of the industry, there must be a general purging, which only the fittest will survive."[6]

Truer words were never spoken but Blackton had no idea when he uttered them that the purging to come would be his own. Once Hampton seated his new directors, one of the first orders of business was to guarantee Blackton $1.5 million (to be paid over a five-year period) and uncollectiously hustle him out of active participation in the organization; he resigned officially in September 1917. At about this same time, Zukor acquired enough support with the board members of Paramount to oust Hodkinson and allow the crafty little producer to replace him with Hiram Abrams, giving Zukor virtual control of his own distribution, an eventuality which Hampton had foreseen and of which he had previously warned Hodkinson.

For awhile, Harry Aitken had been deceived and allowed himself the luxury of believing that Zukor was serious in his offer

---

[5] William Howard Taft's Postmaster General, the President of the New York Metropolitan Street Railways Corporation and the son of Thomas F. Ryan, who at one time had controlled all transportation in New York City.

[6] *New York Times,* March 13, 1916.

of negotiations. After all, there were a dozen expensive lawyers hard at work preparing a preliminary agreement, or so Harry thought, but as time dragged on, he decided that a little under-the-table conniving on his own part would not be out of order; it might just serve to hasten a decision. And so prior to his departure for New York City on March 10, Aitken issued a press release in Los Angeles to the trade papers, stating that contracts had been signed by the interested parties to effect the transfer of Kessel and Baumann's New York Motion Picture Company, with its Key-

In a rare moment of levity, Sennett posed with Louise Fazenda and Teddy in this comic shot. In his early days at Keystone, Mack had figured prominently in the cast of many of his comedies, but by 1915 business was occupying his time almost completely and his comic appearances gradually became a luxury he could not afford. Not much of a comic and less of an actor, his absence from his comedies was no great loss.

When Sennett and Triangle came to a parting of the way, he left his rights to the name Keystone and most of his directors and comic staff with Triangle, who began producing one-reel Keystone Comedies and two-reel Triangle Comedies, starring second-string Sennett comedians like George Binns. A number of these have recently been unearthed and surprisingly enough, they compare favorably with the Sennett Keystones in content and style.

stone, Kay Bee and Domino product, and his own Reliance, Majestic and Fulton Feature Film Company to the Triangle Film Corporation, which would now recapitalize. Kessel and Baumann, of course, had signed nothing of the sort, but kept their silence and when their New York office was queried by interested trade reporters, no confirmation or denial was forthcoming from May Kenny; the two vice-presidents were unavailable for any comment other than to discuss the day's ball game. Aitken also announced that Triangle's feature production would be reduced in quantity and a program of suitable one-, two- and three-reel subjects would now be made available, providing a better balanced offering to Triangle exhibitors.

Two weeks after his return from Los Angeles, Harry finally made himself available to reporters, and when queried about the possibility of the rumored merger between Triangle and Famous Players he confirmed that discussions had indeed taken place. He then went one step further, broadly hinting that while both parties had found mutual interests and that plans for the proposed merger were well under way, Triangle's new course of action made a second look at the entire proposition imperative. He commented, "I believe our capacity for the preparation of the highest class motion picture plays to be unsurpassed. I found the situation in Los Angeles most satisfactory in every respect. The three directors, Griffith, Ince and Sennett, are in frequent conference, and with a view to the improvement of plays, I found them most enthusiastic over the outlook. . . . At the present time, I consider the whole production end of the Triangle Film Corporation in the most satisfactory condition. I do not believe that any other organization is better prepared to furnish the highest class material and this I think is a conservative statement of what I witnessed in Los Angeles. The task of having to supply nearly 1500 separate individual theaters with Triangle Plays has been no small one . . . we will supply 10,000 within the year."[7] Harry's approach at this time was to give the fish plenty of line, act cool and coy, and make them think that he had an ace up his sleeve. It was a dangerous, calculated risk to force Zukor's crowd to show its hand. It was also a bit naive, for the opposition was far and away too clever to be taken in by Aitken's feint to the left.

The next step, according to plan, was another press release, handed out a few days later by Triangle's publicity department, and stating that the merger with Zukor, Lasky and Goldfish had been completely arranged and would be consummated in Los Angeles on either April 26 or 27. A rumored recapitalization of the

---

[7] *The Moving Picture World,* April 1, 1916, p. 144.

Brought to the screen from her smashing success in Ziegfeld's "Follies," lovely Olive Thomas began at Triangle, where she was starred in a series of pictures during 1917–18 that led to her engagement by Selznick. One of his brightest stars, her rags-to-riches rise from a small Pennsylvania coal mining community to fame and fortune on the screen included a marriage to Jack Pickford, but ended in Paris when she took her own life in the early twenties.

Slim Summerville was briefly costarred with little Bobby Dunn (r) in comedies like Villa of the Movies *(1917). Sennett apparently had hopes of creating another comic duo but Dunn failed to catch on with audiences, and while he had a long career on the comic screen Bobby remained one of the obscure and unsung comedians of the silent era.*

two firms in the neighborhood of $25 million would be handled by H. B. Smithers (Smithers and Company) and Oscar Cubelman (Knauth, Nachod and Kuhn). This was Harry Aitken's final card, a last move to force the wily Zukor to put his money where his mouth was. But the little Hungarian shut his mouth tightly, zipped up his pocketbook and sent for Sam Goldfish.

Upon his arrival in New York City, Goldfish quickly slammed the door shut on any such arrangement with a curt denial issued under Paramount's name. He reopened it slightly by adding that for reasons of efficiency, the feasibility of an interchange of facilities and a possible pooling of equipment, personnel and talent was still under study; at no time did he use the word merger. Apparently, Zukor felt he still needed additional information from Triangle before making his move. By June 27, he had obtained and digested all he needed and the following day, Famous Players announced its merger with the Lasky Feature Film Company in a $12 million combination. Sam Goldfish's company was also involved and his reward was the chairmanship of Paramount's board of directors, a prestigious position guaranteed to remove the ubiquitous Goldfish from exerting any possible distracting action on their flank, and one from which the frustrated producer would soon exit in favor of his own company again.

On that day, Harry Aitken felt as though the world had suddenly come to an end; his brother Roy had been right all along—while Zukor had played him for a fool, Harry had lost his last chance to salvage Triangle via a merger. During the negotiations with Zukor and company, Aitken had realized that should the merger proposition fail, there would be very little he could do to save Triangle from eventual bankruptcy and thus made a number of hard decisions concerning his future operations.

Triangle's producers, who had also favored the merger, kept up a brave front in the face of continued adversity; upon his return from an extensive business trip to New York City, where he had learned the real facts of life, Thomas H. Ince was quoted in *The Triangle* as having given an interview to reporters in which he reputedly said, "I understand it has been rumored out here that Triangle is about to disband. I cannot imagine where such twaddle came from, but I can say that Triangle has never been in better financial condition."

8

Cursed by their Beauty

AS THE CREATIVE FOUNDATION OF TRIANGLE CONTAINED THE greatest production talent in the business at the time, it would seem reasonable to expect an unusual number of outstanding films in the Triangle Plays of 1915-17, yet this is not the case. An investigation of the Triangle release schedule brings forth the obvious but often overlooked fact—Griffith, Ince and Sennett had firmly secured their reputations *before* joining Harry Aitken and their greatest successes of this period were not Triangle Plays. Of the Fine Arts productions under Griffith's supervision, none found a position of high regard in cinematic lore. Only the Fairbanks films made in collaboration with director John Emerson and writer Anita Loos are still remembered and Griffith stayed as far away as possible from wherever Doug was working.

It is now generally agreed that D. W. Griffith reached the apogee of his creative career with *Intolerance*. Standing as his lone achievement during the Triangle period, this exceptional production was not released under Triangle auspices. Pressure applied by investors, appalled at the tremendous cost, had forced "The Master" to reach into his own pocket and buy complete control of the picture in order to see it finished. For 1916, costs were phenomenal and historians still disagree about the exact figure, but whether Griffith brought it in for $573,000 or $1.9 million,[1] the film failed to

---

[1] Over the years, a great variety of figures have appeared in print crediting the cost of *Intolerance* at figures up to two million dollars. According to audit figures recently discovered by historian Arthur Lennig, the actual cost was $573,000—a substantial figure but far from the legend. Lennig delivered his findings in a paper presented at the 1969 annual meeting of the Society for Cinema Studies in Los Angeles and will soon publish his findings in a volume on D. W. Griffith.

Billy Armstrong also had a long career in silent screen comedy without creating much of a sensation; Juanita Hansen stopped at Keystone enroute to fame as a Pathé serial queen, lending her attractive presence to several of Sennett's comedies, such as A Royal Rogue (1917).

recoup his investment, costing him control of his creative destiny for several years.

After its successful premiere at the Liberty Theatre in New York on September 6, 1916, *Intolerance* opened in Los Angeles one month later at Clune's Auditorium. Tuesday evening, October 7, 1916, was an occasion which the industry had long awaited—the answers to all the rumors which had surrounded production would now unfold on-screen for all to see. Clune's Auditorium was packed that night—everyone who was anyone in the business attended—and observers still recall the audience as though it had been charged with electricity—a sense of anticipation weighed heavily on all who were there.

The audience was not to be disappointed, for once again D. W. Griffith had proven himself to be a master of technique. The four stories were interwoven through thirteen reels of bold closeups, sweeping action, extreme long shots, opulent extravagance, a spectacular tracking camera shot, dramatic screen framing and many

Weber and Fields in a scene from The Worst of Friends *(1916). The famed stage comics found the Keystone lot a daily threat to life and limb, and while the money was good, they left without regrets when their comedies failed to click with exhibitors and patrons.*

other masterful achievements to make their plea for tolerance. Maitland Davies described the opening night reaction at Clune's in *The Morning Telegram* the following day:

> D. W. Griffith's spectacle *Intolerance,* better known to the people of Los Angeles as *The Mother and the Law,* was presented at Clune's Auditorium last night and repeated the triumphs it had already scored in New York and San Francisco. An audience that filled every nook and cranny in the theatre was simply swept off its feet and at the end of the first act, tendered Mr. Griffith an ovation such as falls to the lot of few men. It was a genuine heartfelt and well-earned tribute and it came from every portion of the audience. There has never been anything presented in the drama, in opera or on the screen of such tremendous scope and it would not be possible to present such a story by any other means than the motion picture. It justifies every claim that believers in the future of the silent drama have made and opens up new vistas, new possibilities which have heretofore been unthought of.

Harry Carr of *The Los Angeles Times* went considerably further in direct praise of the picture:[2]

> With *Intolerance,* David Wark Griffith has made secure his place as one of the towering geniuses of the world. As a medium for expressing art, motion pictures may not stand the test of time, but *Intolerance* is greater than any medium. It is one of the mileposts on the long road of art where painting and sculpture and literature and music go jostling eagerly together.

But critical praise was not all in favor of *Intolerance. Photoplay* pointed out that while the spectacle was grand fun, it was also emotionally void, failing to involve the audience as had *The Birth of a Nation. Variety, The New York Tribune* and many lesser critics took the picture to task for this very fault, and ultimately the audiences across the nation rejected it at the box-office. Unable to recognize and appreciate the full significance of *Intolerance,* the critics had met their match, for Griffith's greatest achievement was not the technical virtuosity with which he played upon the viewer's visual sense, but rather in the breadth of life which he injected into an abstraction—*Intolerance* was the visualization of an abstract concept; its challenge was one of thought.

[2] A few months later, Carr was offered employment at Keystone, editing the *Mack Sennett Weekly.*

True, the film was long, it was overly sentimental, the clearly drawn characterizations were those of absolute good and evil, and in the case of the shorter Biblical and Huguenot sequences, they were emotionally cold, but its main fault seemed to be one of confusion. To follow it carefully and keep up with Griffith required a conscientious attempt to reason, ponder and think, in contrast to the emotional flow which carried a spectator watching *The Birth of a Nation*. Then, as today, audiences went to the movies to be entertained, to relax and enjoy themselves, generally paying little attention to the critical reviews. But those who enjoyed *The Birth of a Nation* were not the same type of audiences who could enjoy *Intolerance* and in this particular case, they found themselves in accord with the critics. Patrons and critics alike seemed unable or unwilling to follow Griffith's lead, especially when the intercutting of stories accelerated as the film was reaching its climax, and so *Intolerance* passed into history as both a major screen accomplishment and a gross box-office failure.[3]

While Griffith was busy with his super-spectacle, Frank Woods had exercised control over the Fine Arts production and picture after picture came out of the lot which failed to compete successfully with the Ince product at the box-office. Using players unknown to the general public and poor stories, the Fine Arts contributions to the Triangle program remain largely forgotten today. No outstanding pictures flowed from this avenue into the Triangle exchanges, and while there were some good ones in the overall schedule, few of the Fine Arts stars managed to earn their keep, with the exception of Douglas Fairbanks. The Fine Arts period even proved to be a rather sterile spot in the career of such stellar attractions as Dorothy and Lillian Gish, who would blossom forth once again under Griffith after leaving Triangle. But during 1915-17, Lillian especially seemed to have been eclipsed by the material she was given. It was not that Miss Gish was unable to cope with

---

[3] Basically pacifist in its approach, the message of *Intolerance* is one of brotherhood and charity. At the time of its release, an emotional alliance with the Allies against the Central Powers was being fostered by moulders of public opinion; historians have speculated that had *Intolerance* been released six months earlier, Griffith would have done much better financially. In the fall of 1919, both the Babylonian and modern sequences were removed from the feature and with a few additions of footage shot but unused in *Intolerance* and with some minor revisions in structure, were exhibited as individual subjects entitled *The Fall of Babylon* and *The Mother and the Law,* during a special Griffith Repertory Season held at New York's George M. Cohan Theatre. Trade reviews given to both of these films were quite favorable, but it is apparent that neither one grossed much money for Griffith. *The Mother and the Law* was already dated by dress and camera technique, with all the trappings of a 1913 melodrama, exactly what it was.

the stories, indeed she gave some fine performances in the Fine Arts pictures. But for the most part, they were program pictures with a psychological motivation which, while artistically done at times, failed to carry audiences along with them. Typical of the Gish Fine Arts films, *The Children Pay,* a 1916 release, told the story of two young girls caught in a cross-fire of their parents' emotional unhappiness. The script temporarily relieved their sufferings by giving one to each parent in a separation, but this unsatisfactory arrangement ended with the eldest marrying a young man in order to take custody of her sister and make a happy home for both. At its conclusion, the viewer was left wondering if this was really the solution after all, or if further unhappiness awaited the girls.

Cross Currents, Helen Ware's first Triangle feature, was typical of the Fine Arts productions and its synopsis from Triangle gives an idea of the type of picture Woods was producing and audiences were shunning:

> A picture of life in society and also of that on a desert isle. Elizabeth Crane (Helen Ware), who lives in Washington, is engaged to a diplomat named Paul Beale (Courteney Foote). Flavia (Teddy Sampson), her younger sister, returns from a Paris school. Beale becomes interested in Flavia, and Elizabeth releases him from the engagement. He marries the young girl. Silas Randolph (Sam de Grasse) invites a party for a cruise on his yacht. His sister and Flavia induce Elizabeth to accompany them. The yacht catches fire, and an explosion destroys the vessel. Flavia is picked up by a sailing vessel. Paul and Elizabeth are washed ashore on a desert isle. Elizabeth nurses Paul, who has been weakened by the adventure. Flavia organizes a searching party and cruises in the vicinity where her husband and her sister are lost. They land on the desert isle and are seen by Paul and Elizabeth. Suddenly leaving Paul, Elizabeth drowns herself.[4]

Fine Arts production was hampered to a degree by a lengthy list of defections from the directorial ranks. The first to leave was one of Griffith's most creative and dependable directors, 28-year-old Christy Cabanne. Cabanne had worked under Griffith for several years and had a flair all his own, best seen perhaps in his earlier *Enoch Arden.* Earning $25,000 yearly with Fine Arts, Cabanne suddenly left the fold to join the new and untried Metro

---

[4] *The Triangle,* Vol. 1, #10, December 25, 1915, p. 3.

While dapper little Charlie Baumann could play the clown if he wished, there were occasions when he assumed the guise of the hard-working motion picture magnate. But much of the time, he exercised his option to let Adam Kessel run the business, content to indulge himself in the good life, such as inspection tours of the corporation's western production activities. This snapshot was taken during a 1915 visit to Keystone while Weber and Fields (r) were filming one of their comedies.

organization in August 1916, where his first assignment was directing Francis X. Bushman and Beverly Bayne, the screen's great love team of that period, in a serial, *The Great Secret*. Cabanne would progress no further as a director and many would argue with some justification that his career went downhill after leaving Griffith. His departure was interpreted by many as a protest against the story assignments given him at Fine Arts.

II

Although Tom Ince produced *The Coward* and a few other above-average stories while at Triangle, the most consistent group of films to come from Inceville and Culver City was the series of William S. Hart westerns. While Ince took credit at the time for Bill Hart's success, it is now generally accepted that Hart himself was the guiding genius, presiding over the production of his films with a minimum of involvement by Ince. Like Griffith, Tom's best remembered achievement of the Triangle era was a super epic which Triangle did not release.

Ince's lengthy record of box-office successes had led the critics to label Tom as a genius of the ordinary, a commercial creature to whom true artistic endeavor was unknown. This reputation hurt Ince deeply, especially while working in harness with the acknowledged Master and the King of Comedy. Preceding Griffith's *Intolerance* to the box-office by five months, his attempt to break the image opened at the Majestic Theatre in Los Angeles on April 17, 1916. Originally entitled *He Who Returned,* its release title carried the all-encompassing designation of *Civilization* and once again, Ince gave the critics fuel for their fires, but unlike Griffith, he turned a handsome profit in the process.

Directed by Raymond B. West, *Civilization* was reportedly shot for a cost of $100,000. Selling territorial rights on the independent market, Ince earned a quick $800,000 and left the distribution to experienced hands like Alexander Pantages, who formed the Western Civilization Corporation to exploit the West Coast rights. But although Tom had sold the exhibition and distribution rights, he did not wash his hands of the film. Three weeks after it opened at the Majestic, *Civilization* underwent extensive surgery, with about 2500 feet (25 percent) of the footage removed and replaced. When the film opened at the Criterion Theatre in New York City for its East Coast premiere, *Civilization* had been strengthened considerably, but not enough to satisfy the reviewers, who took an almost perverted delight in saying, "Ince can make money, but it's not art."

Not as ambitious an undertaking as *Intolerance, Civilization* took war and the resulting effect on humanity as its theme. Taking place in the mythical pastoral kingdom of Wredpryd, the story concerned a young Count Ferdinand (Howard Hickman) who had almost perfected a wondrous submarine to be used against the unnamed enemy of his King. But the Count was a victim of love and the object of his affections (Enid Markey) was deeply involved in the "Purple Cross Insignia of The Mothers of Men Society," a female pacifist movement determined to wipe war from the face of the earth. Ferdinand's refusal to torpedo a steamer led first to mutiny aboard his submarine and then his death. While the King's physicians attempted to retrieve the Count's secrets from his dying brain, Ferdinand's soul met Christ (George Fisher) who returned to Earth in his body. Vividly displaying the raging hell of

Dorothy Gish won a reputation as a light comedienne. Her Triangle Plays like Little Meena's Romance *(Fine Arts, 1916) are not recalled today and her reputation rests mainly on her work in the twenties.*

war before the King's very eyes, "He Who Returned" brought peace forevermore to Wredpryd.

While *Civilization* named no names and pointed no finger specifically, it was interpreted widely as an indictment against war in general, but C. Gardner Sullivan's story very strongly suggested

The Gish sisters, Lillian and Dorothy. Both veteran stage and screen actresses who had joined Griffith at Biograph in the early days of the screen, they won critical acclaim for their many and fascinating portrayals during long screen careers which spanned both the silent and sound eras.

that the culprit was Germany, a contention strengthened by the characters' names and uniforms. In spite of criticism for its allegorical approach to the subject of war, slow pacing, a lack of overall design in the crowd and battle scenes, and the wooden, one-dimensional acting of most of the cast, the many pacifist movements of the time saw the essence of their struggle reflected in *Civilization* and responded with fervor.

At the same time, the film held an appeal for others who leaned toward an anti-German position, and its military scenes (produced with the cooperation of the U.S. Navy) were realistic and even spectacular at times. When the box-office tally was completed, it was apparent that Ince had shrewdly managed to put forth a film that was attracting audiences from both camps, and while time has denied him the critical acclaim Griffith has received for *Intolerance,* his reward was immediate and strengthened an enviable commercial position.

In addition, *Civilization* was credited with helping to re-elect Woodrow Wilson, who campaigned that summer on the slogan, "He kept us out of war," and the value of this publicity was not lost on Ince, who again revamped the film after America went to war in 1917, adding new titles and a prologue containing Wilson's message to Congress.

Civilization had not occupied Ince's time nor his imagination to the extent to which *Intolerance* had involved Griffith, and as a result the producer turned out several interesting films in addition to the Hart series. Typical of Ince's better pictures was *The Coward,* described by Triangle in the following manner:

> The brave Colonel Winslow, veteran of the Mexican War, lives in hope of great future for his only son, Frank. At the outbreak of the Civil War, a recruiting station is opened in the Virginia village where the Winslows live but Frank, obsessed with fear, enlists only after his father has threatened to kill him if he refuses. The very first night on picket duty, the boy deserts and returns home. His father, in shame and humiliation, takes his place in the ranks. Frank hides in the garret when a Union force raids the village and overhears several Northern officers discussing a weak point in their line. Fear departing, he holds them up and gets the plans. Then follows a thrilling ride to the Confederate camp. As he dashes across a bridge, his father, on picket, shoots and horse and rider tumble into the swift current. The boy reaches shore, however and with a knowledge of the enemy's weakness, the Southern troops win a great victory.

Colonel, now private Winslow, is summoned to headquarters and when he learns that his son made the victory possible, the stirring drama ends with their reconciliation.[5]

A simple, fast-moving psychological drama, *The Coward* is still a fine film today, if one can forgive Frank Keenan's brusque overacting as Colonel Winslow. Keenan, a well-known stage star and one of the few of Aitken's experimental group to successfully master the cinema and its techniques, was prone to mugging for the camera but soon overcame this to make a long series of profitable films for Triangle. Charles Ray's portrayal of the cowardly son remains a sensitive and moving interpretation of the eternal interplay and fine line between fear and courage. While the ending was predictable, it pleased audiences who tend to enjoy a happy finish regardless of how incredible it might be and *The Coward* gave Ray's career a large boost toward the brief stardom he would enjoy, all for a negative cost of $17,922.87.

Probably the most popular Ince film of the Triangle period was the story of a hoydenish young society matron who returned to her guardian-uncle's home in Scotland, where the rough edges of her character were tempered to reveal a real woman. *Peggy* starred Billie Burke and William Desmond, and although advertised as a $200,000 production it cost only $58,976 to produce. However its popularity with critics and audiences alike made it the Triangle hit of 1916, if there was such a thing.

But it was the William S. Hart westerns which in great measure account for the lionizing of Tom Ince by film cultists, especially in Europe. Viewed today, the Hart films possess both a simplicity of structure and an understanding of human nature not generally found in the horse operas of 1915-17. In fact, these very characteristics give the modern viewer who is unacquainted with Hart an uneasy feeling that he has somehow missed the reason for the western star's popularity at the time.

In spite of his age, size and previous stage experience, all factors which should have restricted his career before the camera, Bill Hart became the most popular gunslinger of them all. Ince's supervision of the early Hart westerns (1914-15) for Kay Bee, Broncho and Domino quickly brought success and Hart then took over the reins. The western of this period had suffered from an overexposure and redundancy of theme; Hart broke the mold and moved

---

[5] *The Triangle,* Vol. 1, #2, October 30, 1915, p. 3.

Wallace Reid and Dorothy Gish in a light-hearted moment between Triangle Plays. Wally Reid began his career at Vitagraph with his father Hal Reid, but did not really catch fire until after his role as the blacksmith in The Birth of a Nation.

into new pastures with *The Return of Draw Egan, The Aryan* and *Hell's Hinges*. In a sense, the Hart westerns were also repetitive, yet each had its own individual twist and in spite of a maudlin sentimentality which surfaced all too often, Bill Hart achieved a rapport with audiences unmatched by any of his contemporaries, whose efforts offered no serious competition.

Most highly acclaimed by his admirers today, *Hell's Hinges* cost $31,307 and remains a classic example of Hart's best work. Released early in 1916, its uncomplicated synopsis belies the powerful force with which this story of stark calamity moved toward its climax—*Hell's Hinges* was early Hollywood's unwitting translation of Greek tragedy to the screen, via the American West:

> To the tough Western town named Hell's Hinges comes the Reverend Robert Henley and his sister Faith. Silk Miller, the crafty saloon and gambling house keeper stirs up sentiment against the better element. Some rough men and women interrupt the service. Blaze Tracy, a notorious gun man, drives the bunch out of the church when one of the men insults Faith. Silk decoys Henley to his saloon, where Dolly, one of the dancehall girls, induces him to drink until he is intoxicated. Blaze goes away to a nearby town to fetch an organ for the church. On his return, he finds the church burned down, Henley killed and Faith brokenhearted over the disaster that has come to the good element. In fury, Blaze shoots the treacherous Silk, sets the saloon on fire and sees the flames wipe out the town as a result of a high wind. He takes Faith away with him, saying that their future would henceforth lie beyond the mountains.[6]

This thematic emphasis was repeated with varying success in many of Hart's westerns and derived from his stage training. The ability to conceptualize a role in conjunction with his writer gave the stern-faced, rather dogmatic Hart a margin on-screen which made allowance for his stiff, no-nonsense portrayals, and in the process created a legend and several fortunes.

III

Sennett's Triangle years were a transitional period between the knockabout slapstick of the early Keystone and his later, more sophisticated Pathé comedies of the twenties. It was Mack's lot to suffer the failure of Aitken's stage star experiment to a much greater degree than either of his partners, but Sennett profited from the experience; with the exception of Harry Langdon, his

---

[6] *The Triangle*, Vol. 1, #16, February 5, 1916, p. 3.

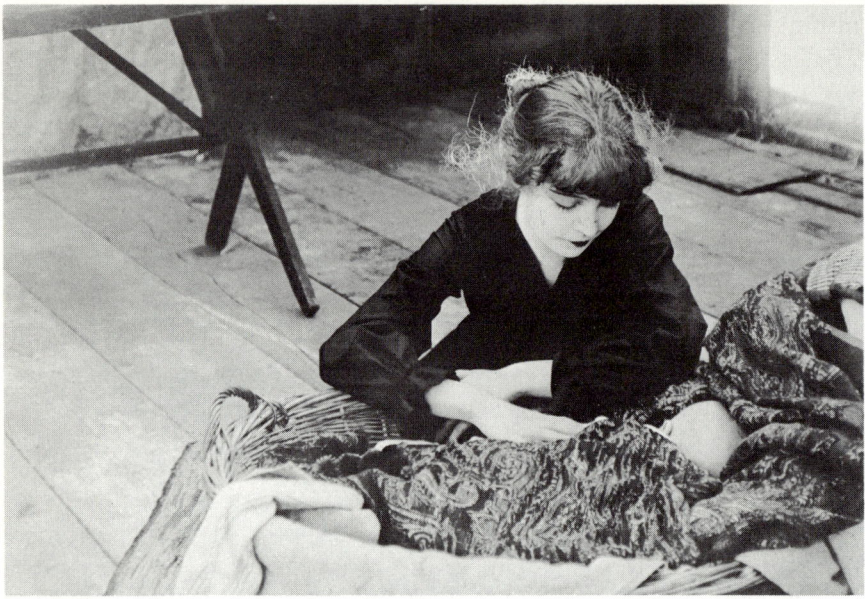

While Lillian Gish made several Triangle Plays which were well-received by critics, as An Innocent Magdalene *(Fine Arts, 1916), her Triangle years did not produce any outstanding roles.*

comics of the twenties all had lengthy screen careers behind them.

His Triangle Comedies were a distillation of all Mack had learned about screen comedy in seven years of acting, directing and producing the unabashed nonsense which sent comedy fans around the world into spasms of laughter. While his identification today with the Keystone period of Mutual release is primarily one of the Keystone Cops and Charlie Chaplin, several of the earlier Keystones were actually minor classics of slapstick, burlesque and parody,[7] but the great majority of these prints had disappeared or worn out long before the intellectuals discovered the "artistry of Keystone."

This was not the case with Sennett's Triangle-Keystone Comedies. Two reels in length (a few longer), more carefully constructed and featuring larger casts, the Triangle-Keystones were widely reviewed during 1915 and early 1916 and physically have better survived the passage of time. A much larger percentage of Sennett's

---

[7] *Mabel's Awful Mistake, A Life in the Balance, At Twelve O'clock* and *That Little Band of Gold.*

Their names lost forever, these nine young ladies were the original Triangle usherettes on duty September 23, 1915, when the first Triangle program was previewed at the Knickerbocker Theatre in New York. Their unusual costumes created quite a stir that evening, but there's no record indicating that the fad caught on with exhibitors.

Triangle-Keystone Comedies are available today for screening than the Ince and Griffith films of this period. Several have now come to be regarded by fans and historians as outstanding examples of Mack Sennett's comic genius.[8] One such was *Mabel and Fatty Adrift*. A variety of versions have circulated down through the years but the original, slightly under three reels in length, contained a dash of just about every cliché associated with comedy, Keystone style. *The Triangle* described it this way:

> Roscoe Arbuckle as a farm boy and Mabel Normand as his sweetheart get married and go to spend their honeymoon by the sea. A rival of Fatty's tries to break into the house but is chased away by Fatty's dog Fido. Assisted by some robbers, the rival knocks the props from under the cottage and launches it on the sea. The couple are awakened by the storm that rages. To keep from drowning, they get on top of the building. The dog Fido is dispatched to shore with a note. He wakes up the parents

[8] *A Submarine Pirate, Bath Tub Perils, His Bitter Pill, Her Fame and Shame, Teddy at the Throttle.*

of Mabel and they get a real estate man to rescue the young folks with his yacht. The robbers have returned to a cafe. During a free-for-all fight, one of the men drops a lighted cigar into a keg of powder, the place is wrecked and the rival and his accomplices are hurled in all directions.[9]

Not so well remembered are the Triangle-Keystones which featured the stage comics, Raymond Hitchcock, Joe Jackson, Eddie Foy, Weber and Fields, Sam Bernard and William Collier. This is quite understandable, for no one of these comedians really had that indefinable touch which made a true Sennett comic and their tenure with Triangle-Keystone was far too short to allow them to build audience rapport, a task which few were actually capable of achieving in front of the inanimate camera.

Several of these comedies were constructed in such a way that the stage comic became little more than a static central figure around which the plot revolved, giving him a minimum to do. A typical example, *Her Painted Hero* (1915), featured Hale Hamilton of Winter Garden fame. In this story of a stage-struck girl (Polly Moran) and her romantic attachment for good-looking men, Hamilton played himself and his important scenes appeared in only three brief sequences. As for what he added to the comedy, which was provided by Charlie Murray, Slim Summerville and Harry Booker, his role could just as easily have been filled by any Joe Doakes. Sennett didn't think that Hamilton was funny, but in this case, he was fortunate; Hamilton didn't like Keystone and returned to the state after completing only one leading role. The real stars of the Triangle-Keystone period were those screen personalities who had learned their trade the hard way and to whom fans paid homage with nickels and dimes—Chester Conklin, Mack Swain, Charlie Murray, Al St. John, Hank Mann, etc.

Early in 1916, Aitken took advantage of Triangle's charter provision allowing it to engage in production and established a comedy company on the Fine Arts lot to provide another series of shorter pictures—the Kay Bee and Triangle Comedies. De Wolf Hopper, who had starred in Triangle's *Don Quixote* (another box-office bust), was paid $1000 weekly to head up the cast, which included John "Shorty" Hamilton and Fay Tincher. To support these stars, Harry drew on Sennett's player roster, using the lesser Keystone actors when they were not busy in the Keystones. Eddie

---

[9] *The Triangle*, Vol. 1, #11, January 1, 1916, p. 7.

Dillon handled the directing chores at first, but soon Mack's assistant directors and second-string cameramen were also involved with the Fine Arts series, making the Keystone lot a beehive of activity during 1916. As most of the personnel involved in these productions were already on the payroll, the Kay Bee and Triangle Comedies were produced at a comparatively slight cost to Triangle.

The many and varied activities at Keystone required the imposition of an organizational structure (as much as it ever could be organized) on a group of free-form improvisors and as the warm camaraderie of earlier days was replaced with a cold and impersonal detachment, Mack's visits to the many sets where shooting was going on became less and less frequent. Cost consciousness became less of a concern than it had ever been before; the New York office begged Sennett to spend more money on his comedies and studio manager George W. Stout obliged Kessel and Baumann by raising the salaries of the minor actors. By padding salaries this way, Stout managed to get the average Keystone Comedy cost up to around $18,000, when it could have been made exactly the same way for $9000. Actors and actresses, comics and comediennes—they came and left with regularity, each hoping to take away more than they had brought. Few accomplished this goal, for the very organization needed to control the growth of Keystone reduced the once-unlimited possibilities for the lightning of stardom to strike. No longer could Mack afford to take a chance on an unknown, as he had done with Arbuckle and Chaplin—it was one hell of a world.

9
How Heroes Are Made

IN KEEPING WITH HIS ANNOUNCED DESIRE TO PROVIDE MOTION picture audiences with a taste of the finest in literature, plays and talent translated to the screen, Harry approached the noted English actor Sir Herbert Beerbohm Tree soon after Triangle was organized. Sir Herbert was asked to spend thirty weeks in front of the Triangle cameras, for which he would receive the then-fabulous salary of $100,000. Although he had appeared in English movies,[1] the actor found it difficult to believe that anyone in his right mind would willingly part with that sum of money merely to point the whirring black box at him, but nonetheless he agreed to accept the offer and the Triangle publicity mill began to spew forth news of the unprecedented signing. But before the contract was finished, Harry would have cause to regret his impetuous offer several times.

Allowed to select his own leading lady, Sir Herbert asked for Constance Collier and Triangle secured her services to support him in his first role. This was a John Emerson adaptation of *Macbeth* and while Griffith rehearsed every scene carefully, it quickly became apparent that Aitken had been victimized; the stage actor had no concept of motion pictures and continually moved out of range or frame, turning his back to the camera and grandly overexaggerating his pantomime. Progress on the picture came to a virtual halt, which failed to perturb the actor, who was on a contract salary instead of a per picture basis, and Harry soon realized that unless something was done quickly, Triangle would be fortunate to complete the single picture within Sir Herbert's six-

---

[1] The National Film Archives in London has a print of Sir Herbert's 1914 version of *Trilby*, made for the London Film Company.

month stay. A hurried call went out for extras and Griffith selected Monte Blue to double the famed thespian in every scene except those in which Sir Herbert's face was recognizable. Blue thus made the majority of the picture masquerading as the star for $30.00 weekly.

Once the picture was finished, Sir Herbert took a leave of absence and went to New York to star in a stage play while Triangle cut, titled and released the magnificent effort. As the reader might expect, the finished picture failed to attract patrons to the theaters, even bombing in London where it was pulled from its ten-week premiere run after only one week. When Sir Herbert returned to Triangle, Harry threatened to break the contract and in an effort to force the actor out, cast him in *Old Folks at Home,* a picture about as far removed from Sir Herbert's talents as could be imagined. His appearance in this potboiler did not come until near the end of the picture, although liberal use of his name was made in its advertising. Sir Herbert, realizing that Aitken was deadly serious, now decided to ask that he be released from his Triangle contract, rather than further antagonize Harry, who was hard at work to find some legal basis for voiding the remainder of it. Harry accepted his offer and Sir Herbert Beerbohm Tree took his leave of Triangle to return to England.

In view of box-office disasters like *Macbeth* and De Wolf Hopper's *Don Quixote,* Triangle was fortunate in having its own established stars to fall back on and none were more popular or respected than William S. Hart, a native of Newburgh, New York, whose early life and travels west of the Mississippi had given him a definite and deep impression of what the old West was really like. Hart came to the movies in 1914, after a career which had carried him from cowhand in real life to stage roles in westerns like *The Virginian,* with a brief stop in Shakespearean plays and critical acclaim as Messala in the original stage company of *Ben Hur.* While pursuing his career, around the turn of the century he had roomed in New York with another aspiring actor, Thomas H. Ince, and his career in pictures was made possible because of this friendship.

Hart had seen and digested a great number of screen westerns, all of which had left a bitter taste in his mouth. "Broncho Billy" Anderson and the up-and-coming Tom Mix were the two leading stars of the day, but Hart felt that even their movies failed to portray the West as he had known and lived it, and anxious to set the record straight, he struck out for California and Tom Ince in

When W. H. Productions was formed in late 1917, its initial reissues made no mention of the original title. Threatened by Federal Trade Commission action, W. H. agreed to a compromise, shown on this Keystone reissue main title. Note the copyright statement, which had no basis in fact—none of the W. H. reissues were actually copyrighted, but this statement was used as a deterrent against unauthorized duping, still a healthy if illegal practice in 1918–19.

the early summer of 1914 after completing his tour in *The Trail of the Lonesome Pine.*

Although reluctant to add another western actor to his company, Ince did agree to Hart's request and cast him as a villain in a couple of two-reelers. When Hart indicated unhappiness with the roles, Ince turned him over to writer C. Gardner Sullivan and director Reginald Barker for two feature films, *The Bargain* and *On the Night Stage.* Pleased about these roles, Hart left for New York to resume his stage career once they were finished, but *The Bargain* proved to be a very good film and Ince recommended it be withheld from Mutual distribution so that a better financial arrangement might be made. Famous Players undertook the distribution and Ince sat on the second feature until *The Bargain* had made Hart's name well-known, at which time *On the Night Stage* became one the Mutual Masterpieces of 1915.

Ince then hired Hart as a director-actor for $125 weekly, a rather low salary for a man whose stardom had been virtually guaranteed before the ink on his contract was dry. This was but the first of several times Ince would take advantage of his acquaintance and as the years passed, their friendship would gradually sour. Now under contract as an Ince player, Hart proceeded to make several two-reelers, bringing them in at little more than $1000 each, including all salaries. These returned small fortunes to Mutual and Ince. *The Disciple,* his first Triangle release, was a five-reel feature costing but $7253, and yet with all his success, Bill Hart's salary remained virtually unchanged. By then, he knew that Ince was using him, but a strong sense of fair play kept the actor from jumping his contract, a factor which allowed Ince to leave Triangle in June 1917 for Artcraft with the promise of bringing Hart with him.

The Hart westerns for Triangle were smooth and polished, lacking the assembly line look one would expect from the frequency of his appearances on-screen. While most were good films, *The Aryan* and *Hell's Hinges* were outstanding for their time and remain even today as classic examples of the genre. Great crowd pleasers wherever and whenever shown, Hart's films gave him a stature equal for a time in the early twenties with Mary Pickford, Charlie Chaplin and Douglas Fairbanks; today he is one of the few silent screen cowboys whose name registers with the general public when it is asked to recall the golden days of the movies. It was Bill Hart and Douglas Fairbanks who carried the burden of the Ince and Fine Arts releases while at Triangle.

When Hart left in 1917, Triangle had no western actor sufficient in stature to replace him in the saddle and one of H. O. Davis' first moves was to switch Roy Stewart from dramatic roles into westerns in hopes that the big actor could carve out a fair share of the market for Triangle. A veteran actor who had broken into movies in 1913 with Aitken's Majestic, the rugged Stewart had joined Triangle in December 1916, replacing Keith Armour in *A House Built upon Sand,* and was reasonably competent before the camera, adept at light comedy as well as deep drama. Cliff Smith, who had worked with Hart, directed Roy's Triangle westerns and Stewart caught on in a series of Hart-like roles, but Triangle was unable to properly exploit films like *The Learnin' of*

Roscoe "Fatty" Arbuckle's grotesque size and agile acrobatics helped make him one of the leading Triangle-Keystone stars. But Arbuckle also possessed a fine sense of comedy, and he wrote, directed and starred in numerous Triangle-Keystone Comedies. His talents were exceeded only by his gross appetite for food, fun and females, and Roscoe was well on his way to a permanent niche in the comedy hall of fame with Chaplin, Keaton and Lloyd when a scandal in 1921 ruined his career completely.

Jim Benton. While Roy's portrayals never had the depth or appeal of Hart, he did turn out to be one of Davis' best money makers.

Douglas Fairbanks was a completely different personality and

Glen Cavender got the point quickly and Roscoe Arbuckle made certain that he didn't forget it in this scene from Fickle Fatty's Fall *(1915). Roscoe took leave of Keystone late in 1916 to produce his own comedies for Paramount, and by 1919 had moved into the comic feature field with great success, but it's as a Keystone comic that he is best remembered.*

one whose early success defied the imagination of many, including Griffith. On-screen, Doug was the personification of the all-American boy, more concerned with how he played the game than if he won it, and an outgoing advocate of physical fitness as a cure for the blues. His early hits came in association with director John

Emerson, who immediately recognized exactly how best to present this ball of active energy to the public. Aided and abetted by a young writer named Anita Loos, Emerson hitched his wagon to the Fairbanks star and rode it far into the heavens.

Fairbanks' contract specified that Griffith was to supervise his films personally, but of course, D. W. did nothing of the sort. While Doug could have broken his contract soon after signing it, he had the sound counsel to remain and learn—the salary was tolerable. Dividing his time between the East and West Coasts, he made Triangle features in both places and watched his brand of boyish charm work its magic on the public, while fending off increasingly attractive offers from other producers. The Fairbanks films of this period are far from his best remembered efforts today, but at the time, *The Matrimaniac, American Aristocracy, Reggie Mixes In, His Picture in the Paper* and others competed with Hart at the box-office, making Douglas Fairbanks about the only real financial attraction on the Fine Arts lot.

Doug's Triangle roles were triumphs for virtue and clean living, and the zestful Mr. Fairbanks directed his attention to then-current fads like psychiatry, which he proceeded to demolish unmercifully with satire. The closest thing to Douglas Fairbanks' performances on the screen during this period would come a couple of years later in the still-emerging comic genius of Harold Lloyd, who added a dash of comedy to many of Fairbanks' themes and approaches during 1918-19. Both became all-time greats of the silent screen—and both were happy-go-lucky screen prophets of optimism dedicated to the proposition that the average American could overcome any adversity.

Other than Hart, Ince had no real stars of the first magnitude, although a promising youngster named Charles Ray was slowly working his way to the top. Sort of a vagabond actor who had spent most of his stage career in traveling stock companies, Ray joined Ince around 1912, and because of his extremely youthful appearance was soon in great demand on the lot, specializing in rural roles with some success. His first big Triangle role, *The Coward,* temporarily took him away from the farm, but it was as the bashful small town boy in films like *The Clodhopper* that Ray became best known. Although he would reach stardom on his own merit by 1920, he could never outrun the type casting.

Frank Keenan and Walter Edwards were two very fine character actors. Keenan came to Triangle in 1915 with the first wave of stage stars; Edwards had been a director-actor with Ince for a number of years and often carried a film solely on the strength of his name and performance. Keenan adapted to the movies easily, and while often criticized for mugging at the camera, he carried an entire series as star during 1917-18. Below these ranks rested a large number of players carried over from the Mutual period who would become better known once they left Triangle, but who added an acting depth to what were otherwise bleak films—Wilfred Lucas, Sam De Grasse, Spottiswoode Aitken, Walter Long, J. Barney Sherry, Williard Mack, Lewis Stone, House Peters, Taylor Holmes, Tom Chatterton and Frank Borzage, to mention but a few—but many were well along in years, and while fine actors heroic starring roles were out of the question.

On the distaff side, there were the Gish sisters, about whom little need be said. They were both very talented and often wasted in Fine Arts films like *Daphne and the Pirates* and *The Tiger Girl,* neither of which numbers among their better roles. Connie and Norma Talmadge, veterans of the early days at Vitagraph, were also with Triangle during 1916 and made a group of interesting little films (*The Missing Link, Martha's Vindication, The Social Secretary*) for Fine Arts which deserved more recognition than they received at the time.

Griffith had a number of heroines molded in the Lillian Gish image. Juanita Horton, a high school junior, walked onto the lot in 1915 looking for work and became Bessie Love. Her first picture was *The Flying Torpedo,* but it was her work with Bill Hart in *The Aryan* which gave her career a distinct boost. After working with Griffith for several years, Mae Marsh came into her own in a series of pictures with Robert Harron before leaving for Goldwyn in 1916. Both actresses performed well under Griffith, but given too many Pickford and Gish-type roles, were never able to establish their own identities, and their careers stalled after leaving Triangle.

Dorothy Dalton's screen career rose and fell with Tom Ince. His infatuation with the attractive Chicago girl, who had gone on the vaudeville stage after graduation from a convent school, began with a Los Angeles stage appearance caught by Ince in 1915. The usual "you ought to be in pictures" routine followed, but Ince was as good as his word and Dorothy appeared as the Queen in *D'Artagnan,* moving right to the top in her next role as Mary Houston, the erring wife in Hart's *The Disciple*. As this picture was released before the former, her first appearance on-screen was that of a leading lady. Ince continued to feed her good roles, as Dot Haldeman in *The Raiders* and Tecolote in Hart's *The Captive God*. By the time she made *Female of the Species,* Dorothy Dalton shared the billing with Enid Markey, a low-powered actress of the Gish school who had practically grown up in Ince films (and would become best known for her role in the first *Tarzan of the Apes* in 1918), and when *The Flame of the Yukon* appeared, the marquee was hers alone.

Another Ince actress turned out to be Triangle's resident vamp. This was the era of Theda Bara, and among her host of imitators Louise Glaum was one of the best. Joining the Ince player roster in 1915 from Universal, Miss Glaum's work in films like *The Iron Strain, The Aryan, The Wolf Woman* and *Idolaters* enhanced her growing reputation as "the other woman." When Triangle suffered its demoralizing paralysis with the loss of Griffith, Ince and Sennett in 1917, she moved to Paralta, but vamping would go out of style in the early twenties, taking her starring career with it.

Probably the most tragic of the Triangle actresses was young Olive Thomas, who after a career touched with lightning would commit suicide in Paris a few years later. Born Oliveretta Duffy in Pittsburgh, she had left home to work in New York City, entered a beauty contest and wound up a star in the Ziegfeld Follies. From there to Triangle and the movies was a short jump and the still-under-age Miss Thomas showed every sign of developing into a sensitive actress when Myron Selznick took over her career.

Belle Bennett, Enid Bennett, Alma Rubens, Seena Owen, Bessie Barriscale and Alice Terry were dependable performers well-known to those who patronized Triangle films at the box-office, but only the youthful Miss Terry would rise to a greater fame in the twenties with her appearances opposite Rudolph Valentino.

The team of Weber and Fields was the most interesting of all the stage comics acquired by Sennett in 1915. Born in 1867, Joe Weber and Lew Fields were both New York City boys who teamed professionally on-stage in 1877. Their world-famous Dutch comedy makeup had been copied by many (including Chester Conklin) and with a stage career spanning 38 of their 48 years, they clearly stood at the top of their profession when approached to join the Keystone Comedies.

Weber and Fields found it hard to believe that Harry Aitken was real; who in his right mind would pay even the greatest bur-

The scrawny little man presented himself to George W. Stout one day in late 1916, looking for work. Stout, busy with his duties as Sennett's studio manager, paid little attention to the applicant, who offered to scrub floors and do carpenter work between comedies. Finally, Stout asked the routine employment question, "What makes you think you're funny?" The little man turned his back, bent over and quickly whirled around, straightening up into Stout's face, but this time with a moustache in place and his eyes crossed. A delighted Stout, who had long wanted Ben Turpin on the Keystone roster, hired him on the spot. Ben appeared in only a small handful of the Triangle-Keystones, but by the twenties, he was Sennett's most popular comic on the lot, drawing a salary of $3000 weekly, a sum exceeded only by Harry Langdon.

Thomas Harper Ince, a frustrated actor from a theatrical family, found his metier in motion pictures. Throwing his lot in with Kessel and Baumann, he moved West to create a reputation with stylistic western films far ahead of their time in story values. A masterful organizer, Ince was responsible for introducing a systematized production technique to movies which freed him from the director's megaphone yet allowed him to stamp each Ince-produced film with his own influence.

lesque comedy team $3500 a week to prance around in front of a camera? They had made a few pictures for the World Film Corporation in 1914, but at a far lower salary, and so when Harry's agent offered to hire them, they would not agree until their own agent reassured both men that Triangle *would* pay what it offered.

Their first week on the lot went by quickly and Friday noon found Weber and Fields first in line at the pay window to receive their check. While Weber collected the envelope, Fields hired a taxi and off they went to downtown Los Angeles, clutching the pay envelope tightly. Spotting a bank at the corner of 6th and Olive, they stopped the taxi and ran in, sliding to a breathless stop in front of a teller's window. Hastily endorsing the check, they shoved it across the window to the teller, who took only one quick look

The Christus (George Fisher) visits the battlefield in a scene from Thomas H. Ince's anti-war epic of 1916, Civilization. *Produced while Ince was a cornerstone of Triangle,* Civilization *was marketed outside the Triangle organization and thus returned a fat profit, as did most Ince pictures, but failed to give him the critical acclaim which* The Birth of a Nation *had brought Griffith. With all due respect to D. W., many would agree that he could have used some of Ince's talent at making profitable pictures a few years later.*

before asking, "How do you want it?" Incredulously, Weber stared at Fields, who stared back in utter amazement, "You mean they're going to give us money for that?" The teller smiled, assuring them the check was good for $3500 cash; if they would only tell him what denominations they wanted, he'd cash it for them. Still staring at each other, the two comics mumbled about identification and the teller laughingly replied that everyone knew Weber and Fields, especially when they were still in full makeup. Sheepishly, the comics realized that they were putting on a free show for the customers, who applauded loudly. Greatly relieved to find that the Keystone check was good after all, Weber decided that they really didn't want cash, but would open an account instead.

Everyone on the Keystone lot loved Joe and Lew, whose innocence toward the movie business made them the best inadvertent jokesters in screen comedy. Watching their rushes with Sennett one day, they overheard him complaining to director Frank Griffin about static electricity marks on the footage. Not understanding that the Pathé camera was especially prone to causing static electricity images to register on the film, but seeing the jagged streaks across their pictures on the screen, the two comedians rushed out of the screening room for the dispensary, where they anxiously begged for a cure for "the statics."

Had Weber and Fields been as funny on-screen as off-camera, their stay in the land of gold might have lasted far longer, but primarily dependent upon dialogue in their comedy skits, and not accustomed to the everyday hazards of Keystone life (they were nearly killed when a car in which they were riding in a chase scene tipped over), Weber and Fields were most agreeable to the suggestion their contract be cancelled when their pictures failed to meet with exhibitor favor. While in years to come, Joe and Lew would joke about their Keystone days, both men had the "fear of God" instilled in them by their experiences that summer of 1915 and not even $3500 a week was sufficient to keep them risking life and limb in Triangle-Keystone Comedies—the stage was safer and both lived to celebrate their 74th birthday.

The other stage comics did not work out as well, although Raymond Hitchcock did develop into a better screen comic than his early roles indicated. But for the most part, Sennett's comedies maintained their reputation of superiority through the efforts of veterans Chester Conklin, Mack Swain, Charlie Murray, Louise Fazenda and a host of comic supporting characters like Alice Davenport, Phyllis Allen, Al St. John and Hank Mann.

Katherine Kaelred was brought to the screen in The Winged Idol *(Ince, 1915), the story of a fanatical woman who resolved to cure a wealthy young drunkard (House Peters) and did—but he remained devoted to his wife (Clara Williams). It cost $9,310.61 to produce.*

After his role in The Coward *brought Charles Ray to public attention, he became one of Tom Ince's most popular stars with roles like the opium eater in* The Dividend *(Ince, 1916), with Ethel Ulman.*

There was no real lack of talent on the various Triangle lots but the story properties left something to be desired, especially those from the Fine Arts studio (some Triangle executives felt that Frank Woods wouldn't have recognized a good story if it knocked him over) and the limited distribution of the resulting films severely hampered their box-office potential. Had this restriction been removed before Triangle product became tainted goods in the exhibitors' viewpoint, the story we are about to continue might have taken a different direction.

10
Stout Heart but Weak Knees

BY OCTOBER 1916, TRIANGLE'S COMPETITIVE POSITION HAD deteriorated to a point where it appeared that operating capital would shortly be a thing of the past. Even conservative estimators whispered that the firm's capability to continue production and distribution of product would not extend into 1917, unless something radical could be done to improve its cash-on-hand balance. Creditors were knocking on the doors for payment of overdue loans and the bankers were seriously considering attaching their own auditors to Triangle in an effort to reduce costs and funnel off the resulting savings; only Harry's vehement protests forestalled this move. Triangle stock, which had once brought almost $9.00 on an opening price of $5.00, was now selling for $2.00 per share, if and when a buyer could be found. Having borrowed from one to pay another for most of his motion picture career, Harry had already put out feelers to size up the situation, but it was apparent that a recapitalization and new stock issue were out of the question; no other financial houses would touch it.

The Triangle theater concept had died months before; no revenue was forthcoming from this portion of the withering empire. Closing the theaters had done little to improve the corporation's condition and now Harry's appraisal of the worsening situation convinced him that undesirable as it might be, a further retrenchment was in order. Accordingly, he made two moves in October which were to have a dramatic impact on Triangle's future, forestalling the inevitable disaster for another year and prolonging his own grief.

The first, and perhaps the wisest move, was one that should have been taken months before; Triangle opened its doors to the independent exchanges, allowing them to carry Triangle product. In effect, this meant that theaters not directly contracted to Triangle for the entire program could now book and use those portions of the program which they might select as having box-office potential for their particular locations. But this was a case of too little, too late. Triangle product had gained an unenviable reputation by this time among exhibitors and the stampede of independent exchanges to take advantage of this new and liberal policy was not one calculated to overwhelm the organization. In addition to a smaller than anticipated response to this move, the actual cash benefits did not show up on the books in quantities sufficient to relieve the immediate needs for several months.

Tied closely to this policy and more important to Triangle's future was Aitken's decision that his exchange system must go on the auction block. The half-million dollar luxury had not managed to pay its own keep, to say nothing about returning a respectable profit on the huge investment. Disposing of the exchanges meant turning an unprofitable asset into cash, Triangle's most pressing need, and cash would provide token payments for the impatient creditors, in addition to allowing enough operating capital to continue production for several more months. Accordingly, Triangle announced in October that it was seeking experienced exchangemen to buy and operate one or all of the Triangle exchanges.

The original idea had been to dispose of each exchange to a local citizen of the city in which the exchange was located. The contract would bind the new owner to distribute Triangle product, guaranteeing an outlet for the program. Without this clause, it would have been entirely possible for Aitken to sell all 22 of the Triangle exchanges and then find himself with 22 new owners having no desire to link themselves to his product, drying up Triangle's distribution completely. The discouraging aspect of this move was brought to light almost immediately when Harry discovered that his announced willingness to dispose of the exchange system failed to meet with a rash of offers to buy. And so, putting on his hat and coat, Harry Aitken went out into the street looking for someone to take the distribution of Triangle product off his hands and put some cash in his pocket.

The answer to his problem came in the person of William W. Hodkinson and an organization in the process of capitalization which the imaginative Hodkinson was fond of calling Superpictures. Forced out of Paramount by Zukor and Lasky, Hodkinson

One of Adolph Zukor's original imports from the stage in 1913, House Peters came to Triangle after a short stay with World in 1915, playing both leads and heavies. Triangle roles for Ince did little to advance his career and Peters soon left to continue a lengthy career which included starring roles, and later, many delightful character parts.

had vowed that he would one day humiliate the little Hungarian in full and set his active mind to work looking for a way to beat Zukor at his own game. He found the vehicle for his revenge in

A youthful Jack Gilbert was a permanent fixture in the Ince dramas during the Triangle years, starting his career at sixteen as a bit player at $2.00 a day. He left Triangle to become Maurice Tourneur's assistant but eventually returned to acting with Fox and Goldwyn. Irving Thalberg cast Gilbert in The Big Parade *(1925) and John Gilbert turned into one of the hottest male properties since Valentino had arrived in 1921— and it all started with Ince.*

A hard-drinking vaudeville favorite, "Shoeless" Joe Jackson was the only comic on the Keystone lot allowed to keep liquor in his dressing room. Although he alone had Sennett's permission to imbibe during working hours, Joe was unable to laugh or drink his way to screen fame, but he did manage to last longer than most of the other stage comics in Sennett's employ. This touching scene with Betty Marsh came from Gypsy Joe *(1916).*

an enterprising neophyte in the celluloid jungle, Frederick L. Collins of the McClure Publications. McClure had formed its own motion picture production company, and on its behalf Collins had naively tendered an offer to buy into Famous Players. Leading him by the nose on a path similar to the one which Harry Aitken had followed, Zukor had toyed with Collins until the time to make a decision arrived, then folded up his tent and walked away, leaving an angry Collins looking very much for all the world like one who had been taken to the cleaners. If there was one thing which Collins couldn't stand, it was being made to play the court jester out in the open where everyone could chuckle at him.

As a result of this experience, a sadder but wiser Collins joined forces with Hodkinson and together they established a new distribution arrangement in November. Formed under the laws of the State of Delaware, Superpictures Incorporated was capitalized at

$9 million; $6 million in preferred stock and $3 million in common stock. Hodkinson became president of the new organization and Collins took the vice-presidency. Holland S. Duell of Duell, Warfield and Duell represented the financial backing in the post of Secretary and Raymond Pawley, Zukor's former treasurer and another disgruntled ex-Paramount employee, became Superpicture's treasurer. These four men also formed the Board of Directors.

Needing a means of distribution, Hodkinson carried on a behind-the-scenes dialogue with Aitken, and gained a verbal agreement to acquire the Triangle exchange system before formally announcing Superpictures to the trade. For Harry Aitken, Hodkinson's new venture had been another one of those heaven-sent strokes of good fortune which had dogged his footsteps for a decade. Superpicture's offer of $600,000 for the 22 exchanges meant that Triangle had slipped out from under an unprofitable harness, acquiring enough cash to satisfy the immediate requirements of both creditors and production. The relief which Harry felt at this development gave

A beer garden scene from Old Heidelberg *(Fine Arts, 1915) which starred Wallace Reid as Prince Karl. Reid shortly left Triangle to become a matinee idol at Paramount and in 1923, died of narcotics addiction.*

him the appearance of a man ten years younger on November 18, when the Triangle Distributing Corporation was officially announced to the public. For the first time since he had started the merger negotiations with Zukor, the harried promoter began to look himself again, losing the wan and tired look of a man fighting desperately for his life. Hodkinson assumed the posts of president and general manager of Triangle's new distributor and Aitken had an iron-clad guarantee that his product would not be locked out of the market place.

Actually, Superpictures could not have existed had it not been for Aitken's willingness to place Triangle's distribution in its hands. Although the announced aim of the new company had been one of acquiring the finest of available films for marketing, the major firms were not about to surrender their profitable operation to Hodkinson and he would have been left to scrounge the independent production field for product, a rather unhealthy prospect in 1916. But Triangle's problems, coupled with Hodkinson and Collins' desire to even a score with Adolph Zukor, made Superpictures possible and Harry viewed the Triangle Distributing Corporation as having removed several problems from his shoulders. Actually, it was to bring more new troubles than the old ones it relieved, mainly in the person of one Stephen A. Lynch.

In view of all the romantic hokum that has been passed off concerning the early days of movie making, it is often difficult to accept the fact that the motion picture industry had its own versions of Al Capone and Dutch Schultz, long before prohibition brought national notoriety to hoodlums of this kind. But Stephen A. Lynch personified this exact concept and exhibitors in the southeastern United States who had occasion to come into business contact with Lynch in the 1914-18 period still turn livid with rage at the mere mention of his name, even after more than a half-century.

From his headquarters in Asheville, North Carolina, Lynch had built up control over a chain of about thirty theaters in the principal cities of the Carolinas, Georgia, Alabama and Florida, forming the S. A. Lynch Enterprises. A measure of respectability had been granted his activities earlier, in the form of an appointment by Hodkinson as the sole southeastern distributor of Paramount Pictures and Lynch took full measure of this valuable distribution franchise to parlay his theater chain into a position of almost unlimited power in the exhibition field. Lynch and his stooges would move into a city or town and approach the local theater owner with a proposition to play Paramount product, usually at a price considerably above what the exhibitor was paying for competing product.

If the exhibitor bought the package with no questions, all went well, but if he refused or played coy, hoping to strike a better bargain, Lynch or his operatives dropped open threats to build or buy a theater which would then play Paramount films, undercutting admissions and running the recalcitrant exhibitor out of business. If an exhibitor refused to knuckle under at this point, the unhappy theater man who had faced up to Lynch usually found his business establishment destroyed by dynamite in the dark of night, or literally torn apart by a rowdy crowd hired to do just that. Paramount pictures would span the earth, even if Lynch had to oversee the delivery of each one personally.

Although only one of a number who used such tactics in attempting to gain an exhibition monopoly for Paramount (and for themselves as regional distributors) around the country, Lynch was perhaps the most energetic and certainly the most notorious, delivering the greatest number of contracts to Paramount. Interestingly enough, these underhanded methods were used with the full knowledge and tacit approval of Zukor, who was determined that one way or another, he would rule the industry from production through exhibition. And thus this unsavory character was now brought into the Triangle Distributing Corporation by Hodkinson as a partner.

In the closing weeks of December 1916, a series of single reel Keystone Comedies were announced to the trade, to be available through Triangle exchanges to all exhibitors who wished to book them, regardless of affiliation or non-affiliation with Triangle. This move on Harry's part was the result of an attempt to force a compromise between Mack Sennett and himself. Aitken had decided that a reduction in the length of the Triangle program was necessary both from a production and distribution viewpoint. As he proposed to cut the fourteen reels distributed weekly to twelve, the economy had to be effected somewhere and certainly the five-reel features could not be reduced in length. Sennett's cost factor for the double reel comedies had risen considerably in the past eighteen months, partially because of Aitken's earlier insistence that his producers spend more money on their pictures. In addition to higher salaries, to which he was now committed, Sennett was caught in a general cost spiral, which was affecting the entire industry, and as a result of these factors, Mack was now spending an average of $20,000 per comedy. Only the clever photographic effects and shortcuts devised by cameraman Frank Williams had kept the costs from rising further. While Harry was no miser when it came to spending cash to get what he considered to be a good product, Aitken was now convinced that the answer was to be found in one-reel comedies.

Sennett had argued vociferously that his production capability was now firmly established around the two-reel comedy format and that any attempt to cut back to a single reel would not only interfere with a smoothly operating assembly line, but could not possibly save the amount of money Aitken desired. At the same time, Mack made clear his displeasure with the restrictive Triangle booking policy of the past and claimed with considerable justification that his Triangle-Keystone Comedies were not earning as much as they should due to Triangle's mishandling of the merchandise. As a final measure, he claimed that his dominant position in the field of screen comedy was due in good measure to his evolution from split to full and then to double reels. For "The King of Comedy" to return to single-reel comedies at a time when they were already beginning to pass from the scene would have been injurious professionally to him.

The result of lengthy negotiations and healthy table-pounding was a decision by Harry Aitken to exercise again the production authority granted Triangle in its charter. Sennett's comedies would remain two reels in length, but Triangle would create a production unit capable of turning out single reel comedies for use with the Sunday and Thursday feature releases. These would be sold as Keystone Comedies while Mack's two-reelers remained as Triangle-Keystone Comedies. The establishment of such a unit could most easily be accomplished using the facilities already in existence and so Sennett agreed to a procedure quite similar to that used earlier in the production of the Hopper and Tincher short subjects. His lesser-known directors would handle the task of producing the new series of one-reel Keystones and comics not on call for his regular productions would be made available, as would sets and working space. However, he disclaimed all responsibility and credit for the resulting comedies and the financial end would be handled by Harry Aitken's people, not by his administrative staff.

By this time, Hodkinson had found himself in the unenviable position of having to show a profit or produce a good reason why one was not forthcoming. In the months since the transfer, the

1

Charles Ray (1) had appeared in Ince films for several years when he was cast as the son who deserted from military duty in The Coward *(Ince, 1915), a Civil War drama. Ostensibly a Frank Keenan (2) picture,* The Coward *raised Ray to stardom for his moving and sensitive performance as the lad who tells his proud father that he does not wish to enlist (3) but is sworn into service against his better judgment (4). This touching farewell (5) would soon be replaced with one of desertion but redemption was only two reels away.*

Triangle Distributing Corporation had failed to show a glimmer of the growth predicted by its backers and Hodkinson faced the growing demand that he produce profits by reorganizing his forces. Appointing Robert W. France as his new general manager, Hodkinson now had a buffer between himself and his critics; let France do the explaining while he concerned himself with finding a solution to his dilemma.

2

3

4

5

The unvarnished truth of the matter was a simple one on the surface; while the sale of the Triangle exchange system to Super-pictures had produced $600,000, which was applied to Triangle's most pressing debts, the production costs were still too high to make a satisfactory profit with Triangle's limited distribution. But there was another side to the problem known only to Harry and a select few within the Triangle Film Corporation, and had Hodkinson known the real truth, he would not even have bothered to try.

Triangle films were now available to any exhibitor and independent exchanges were also carrying the Triangle product. A variety of reorganizational patterns had been tried and found to be wanting—the situation was still precarious. In a conference with Harry, Hodkinson pointed out that the Triangle producers were not sharing equally in the adversities which had been a part of Triangle's way of life from its very beginning. Aitken readily agreed and so on February 20, 1917, it was announced that the drawing accounts of flat rate payments to Griffith, Sennett and Ince would be discontinued in favor of a per film percentage basis on a sliding scale. The public relations department announced to the trade that the three Triangle producers would no longer be "deprived" of sharing proportionately in the great financial success of their Triangle pictures, but Griffith, Sennett and Ince knew differently; they were no longer to be fortunate in avoiding a direct share of Triangle's failure. This sort of arrangement did not hit Sennett as hard as it did the other two, as his comedies were the most desired feature of the weekly Triangle program. But Mack was in agreement with the others; Triangle had now become as great a cross to bear as had Mutual before it. Something had to give.

11
The Late Lamented

KESSEL AND BAUMANN WERE IN COMPLETE AGREEMENT WITH THE general philosophy expressed by the man who had so successfully guided their Keystone Film Company for four years, winning an enviable place in the industry for its product. In fact, Baumann had openly hinted throughout 1916 that unless things took a turn for the better, he would jump ship, leaving Harry Aitken to pilot the uncharted waters by himself. Sensing the beginnings of open dissension in his own quarters, Harry was both relieved and dismayed when Kessel and Baumann approached him in late 1916 to announce that their New York Motion Picture Company was about to be placed on the open market; whoever had their price could have the entire operation—lock, stock and barrel. This particular move could have proven disastrous to Triangle—suppose that Adolph Zukor chose to buy them out? Shuddering to himself at the mere thought of such a calamity, Harry asked for a few weeks to think over his course of action and immediately went looking for funds; it cost him $500,000 of Triangle's money to gain title to the New York Motion Picture Company, including its Kay Bee, Broncho, Domino and Keystone films past and present.

Ad Kessel and Charlie Baumann had made a very wise move. When the final crash came, both were somewhat hurt financially by their retention of Triangle stock, but had they not sold the New York Motion Picture Company, they would have been reduced overnight to paupers, with all of the gains of a decade in business wiped out. A weary but determined Adam Kessel remained active in Triangle affairs, but Charlie Baumann retired officially on

162

A stage actress from the Mid-West, Dorothy Dalton came to Los Angeles for an engagement and was seen by Thomas Ince, who personally paved her way into pictures and guided her to the top with one important role after another in Ince films. After enjoying a prominence on the screen as an Ince and Paramount star in the twenties, Miss Dalton left the screen and married into a famed theatrical family, the Hammersteins.

January 31, 1917; the sale of their holdings was consummated in March.[1]

[1] While Baumann retired officially from Triangle, he did not leave the industry. The Kessel-Baumann Picture Corporation was formed with Charlie as president to exploit independent pictures. Never particularly active, it handled such product as the Yankee Photo Corporation's *Headin' Home* (1920) starring Babe Ruth, but ultimately proved to be the instrument which broke up their lengthy association. Curiously enough, neither man trusted the other and when the Kessels discovered that Baumann's wife Annie had received $2970 of company funds for 300 shares of its stock she had turned over to Charlie in April 1921, they filed suit against him, bringing the long partnership to a close.

Things had started happening quickly in 1917 and Harry, always the executive who worked long hours each day, now learned the real meaning of "burning the midnight oil." The pace of exhibitor desertions from the Triangle fold had accelerated in late 1916 at an alarming rate. Typical of the hard-luck stories which eventually landed on Aitken's desk was that of William H. Kemble. Kemble had gained his foothold in motion picture exhibition on the strength of profits made from showing *The Birth of a Nation*. Determined to continue his good fortune, Kemble plowed his earnings into the William H. Kemble Theatre Corporation in 1915, signing a $750,000 contract with Triangle. Leasing the Crescent Theater in Brooklyn, Kemble reopened it as the Brooklyn Triangle Theatre. His business interests expanded with the establishment of the Big T Film Corporation, a sub-exchange with an exclusive contract to distribute Triangle Plays to other Triangle contractors in Brooklyn.

Claiming 100 of the 400 theaters in Brooklyn as his clients, Kemble was the featured attraction on page one of the April 1st (1916) edition of *The Triangle*. The bold headline read OWNER OF BROOKLYN TRIANGLE RIGHTS CONTROLS TWENTY PER CENT OF BUSINESS IN HIS TERRITORY. This was followed in slightly smaller type by "W. H. Kemble, Who Was One of the First to Sign a Triangle Contract and Which Involves More Than Half a Million Says He Is Not Only Making Money Out of His Model Theatre, But Also Getting Big Returns From Rentals and Is Doing Better Than Two of His Competitors Combines." After the usual background material on Kemble and his association with Triangle, appropriately spiced with superlatives concerning his wise decision to associate himself with Triangle Plays, the article arrived at an interesting insight into what had happened to Triangle contractors:

> Kemble went on to explain that some of his customers had tried to leave the fold soon after signing with him for Triangle Plays, citing in particular one exhibitor who argued: 'Mr. Kemble, I'll have to cancel, beginning next week. I have been losing money with Triangle. Something is wrong. It isn't the pictures, for they are the finest made. But somehow they don't draw. People do not come to see them. And so long as people will not come the pictures are worthless. When I took Triangle, I had an idea that all I would have to do would be sit in the box office and take in the money. While my receipts show that I am making as much as when I was running other films, still in view of the fact that I am now paying more than twice as much as I ever paid for service, I cannot somehow show a profit on my books,

commensurate with the amount I have invested and the time I spend around the theatre.

While the article went on to credit Kemble with retaining this particular exhibitor as a customer by stepping in and reorganizing his operation to increase efficiency and improve its general appearance, one can brush aside the flag-waving to arrive at a glimmer of truth which appears in the exhibitor's complaint, as published, thus gaining an insight into why the Triangle program was failing. The Triangle Plays had not increased his business, but their additional cost had eaten heavily into his profits, a situation which can safely be assumed to have been a common complaint. And if Kemble were adept at reorganizing his customer's operations to keep them from leaving Triangle, few exhibitors were fortunate enough to have someone of his caliber looking after their interests.

He must have been so busy servicing their accounts that he failed to pay sufficient attention to his own operation, for as Triangle's flame flickered ever dimmer, Kemble's future took on the unhealthy coloration of bankruptcy. Big T was finally caught taking deposits for which it failed to deliver films and the Triangle Distributing Corporation was forced to pacify the hue and cry raised by the Brooklyn exhibitors, whose complaints had been so long ignored, by withdrawing its franchise. The end came in March 1917 when Kemble could no longer pay his debts. His one recourse was to sell out to the only interested party, Paramount. This story was repeated so often in early 1917 that Harry could almost predict the weekly failure rate blindfolded.

On March 11, D. W. Griffith severed his connection with Triangle, and six days later he signed with Zukor's Artcraft Pictures. "The Master," deep in debt and dark of spirit, realized that his association with Aitken could no longer provide him with either the money or creative challenge he needed to keep going; Zukor offered both. Triangle began to lurch dangerously to one side. Two months earlier, the very popular Douglas Fairbanks had exercised a clause in his contract which guaranteed personal supervision of his pictures by Griffith, and a few days later he surfaced at Artcraft, where Zukor paid him $10,000 weekly, a sum Triangle could not possibly have matched.

Tom Ince took over the production responsibilities at Fine Arts, shutting down the studio and moving all Triangle feature production to his Culver City plant. An East Coast studio was opened

A main identification title from a Triangle release of 1916. Note the extensive use of the Triangle logo.

on Riverside Avenue in Yonkers. The estate of one Clara Morris had been purchased for this purpose and Harry, along with Charles Parker, moved his executive offices from the Brokaw Building to the twenty-room mansion; Kessel and Baumann had returned to their suite at the Longacre Building some months before. Hastily constructed studio facilities were erected in Yonkers and Allan Dwan moved East to accept the production responsibilities there under Ince's administrative supervision.

On April 30, 1917, Triangle announced that it was abolishing the deposit system, long a sore spot with exhibitors. Arrangements had been made with the Fidelity and Casualty Company of New York to underwrite exhibitor contracts for a premium amounting to one percent of one month's deposit. Those exhibitors who did not wish to avail themselves of this new arrangement were free to

When S. A. Lynch Enterprises was awarded the Triangle franchise for the southeastern United States, its own logo replaced that of Triangle on all advertising and even on the films themselves exhibited within the geographical area. This lobby card was used to announce the arrival of Jim Grimby's Boy *(Ince, 1916) to theater patrons.*

continue paying deposits, but all others were allowed to apply their deposits of record against current rental fees.

Meanwhile, Stephen A. Lynch had been continually pressuring Hodkinson at Triangle Distributing, demanding increased profits. The harassed executive responded by blaming the Triangle films, an explanation which the impatient Lynch refused to accept as the sole reason. To prove their point, a weary Hodkinson and Raymond Pawley resigned on May 25. Elated by the opportunity with which they presented him, Lynch purchased their Triangle Distributing stock with his personal funds, and by so doing bought himself the presidency of the organization. C. E. Holcomb became treasurer, Fred W. Kent was named secretary and Frederick L. Collins sent downstairs as the executive head of McClure Pictures, which had been no earth-mover at the box-office. Robert France remained as a member of the Board of Directors, but relinquished his post as general manager. After a careful study of the books and the many ramifications which accompanied them, Lynch suddenly realized that he had been taken to the cleaners. Hodkinson and Pawley had been telling him the truth all along—Triangle films simply were not earning money in sufficient quantities to show an upward profit pattern.

Now the plot began to thicken visibly, for across town at Universal City, H. O. Davis had submitted his resignation to Carl Laemmle in May, clearing the way for his signature on a Triangle contract. In June, he was elected a vice-president and officially appointed as general manager of the Triangle Film Corporation. The production of Fine Arts films, which Ince had shifted to his Culver City lot, was moved back to the reopened Fine Arts studio and Davis instituted a severe economy wave. Many expensive player contracts were either cancelled or bought up and a consolidation of production was effected in the assembly line manner of Universal. But his very success in putting Triangle back on its feet would partially prove to be his undoing, for Davis had outsmarted Aitken at his own game—self-promotion—and in Harry's book, that was the cardinal sin—never top the boss.

H. O. Davis was a peculiar sort of individual—secrecy was one of his most successful tools. Very few if any in the industry actually knew what his initials represented; his passion for privacy extended into his own personal life and Davis insisted that all refer to him only as H. O. He told few what he planned on doing and ran the studio with the help of two trusted lieutenants brought with him from University City. A highly competent organizer whose background included the promotion of several large fairs, carnivals and exhibits, Davis had been brought into the motion picture business by Laemmle for this very talent. Davis was earning $300 a week (Laemmle was no Santa Claus either) when he began to promote a move to Triangle, but he had a reputation which would justify more money. Finding Aitken receptive to his advances, Davis then played hard to get, a ploy which Aitken should have recognized as one of his own favorite moves, but didn't—such an attitude was one of Harry's weaknesses and his pulse never failed to quicken when someone resisted his offers.

In the meantime, Davis saved his weekly paychecks for three consecutive weeks and returned them to the Universal paymaster, asking for a single draft in the amount of $900. Over lunch with Aitken a few days later, Davis was prepared to back up his claim when Harry brought up the question of what salary would be involved should the move take place. Davis nonchalantly mentioned that such a move should be worth an increase in pay, to which the good Mr. Aitken readily agreed. The $900 check was then produced and represented as his last paycheck. The two men then agreed upon $1500 a week as a fair price and shook hands; Davis would join Triangle as its new general manager as soon as he could arrange his exit from Universal.

Harry was not to find out for several months that he had been conned for a $1200 weekly increase instead of the $600 he thought he was paying. When he did discover the deception, the enraged promoter was ready to fire his new manager, but caution prevailed —Davis had a firm one-year contract which would have cost Harry well over $60,000 to cancel. He decided instead to accept his mistake and let Davis finish out the year, but there was nothing in the book which insisted he refrain from informing H. O. of his great displeasure, an act in which Aitken engaged whenever the two men met.

Fourteen-year-old Bessie Love was one of Triangle's bright young ingenues. Her promising career began under Griffith, but once she left "The Master," Bessie found herself cast in roles which denied her use of her talents and although a popular actress during the twenties, she never really lived up to her early potential.

Hale Hamilton came to Keystone in 1915 direct from a successful Winter Garden appearance. Hamilton starred in only one Triangle-Keystone Comedy, Her Painted Hero (1915), playing a stage actor admired by Polly Moran. Screen veterans Charlie Murray and Slim Summerville carried the comedy, with Hale appearing as the object of Miss Moran's affections. This is a frame enlargement from that Keystone.

The month of May also found Ince and Sennett in New York City. As a result of the lengthy and bitter conferences which took place in late May and early June, Ince summarily withdrew from Triangle, selling his 26 percent holdings in the corporation back to Triangle for a sum which was reported to be between $250,000 and $750,000, depending upon whether you believe Ince or Triangle's announcement. Sennett would withdraw in late June, leaving the fabled Keystone name behind him.

Upon learning of the corner into which his greed had backed him, Lynch reorganized the Triangle Distributing Corporation once again in June. His brother became vice-president and Y. F. Freeman replaced Collins as a director; the executive head of McClure Pictures now moved down to the presidency of Superpictures, with Conrad Milliken as his vice-president and Robert France as secretary and treasurer. With 50 percent of Triangle Distributing's common stock and Superpictures' preferred stock in his hands, Stephen A. Lynch was now undisputed master of both organizations and their destiny, the thought of which chilled him after he realized that Hodkinson and Pawley had actually told him the truth all along.

Immediately after consolidating his hold on Triangle Distributing, Lynch put a new booking plan into effect in June. To secure sufficient feature pictures to continue a two-release-per-week schedule, Triangle had recently fallen back on its vault. Old Hart and Fairbanks features were reissued with the slogan, "The Good Ones Never Die." Theaters were now allowed to (1) book the new releases as special pictures at regular prices[2] or (2) rebook Triangle reissues at a cost amounting to 50 percent of the price they had originally paid. If neither the special nor a reissue appealed to him, the exhibitor was allowed to go into the open market without penalty to find a suitable picture to play in place of the Triangle special. This last provision considerably weakened the once-strong grasp that Triangle had maintained over its contractors, setting the stage for a temporary but wholesale desertion in its exhibitors' ranks.

But Lynch had prepared for his own financial exit should the going get too rough. From its very outset, S. A. Lynch Enterprises had been a legitimate business arrangement. Some stock had been sold in the past to raise additional operating capital and the corporation had its own board of directors, of which Lynch was Chairman as well as President. Lynch simply took his Triangle Distributing stock to the S. A. Lynch Enterprises' board of directors, offering to share his magnificent good fortune with them. With his brother voting on his side, the board really had very little opportunity to refuse the offer and on September 10, 1917, Lynch regained his own investment, along with a rather substantial profit for his "wisdom and foresight" in thinking of the organization instead of only himself.

As a large stockholder in Triangle Distributing, S. A. Lynch Enterprises was granted the distribution franchise for the southeastern United States (much as it had for Paramount earlier) and the Triangle product which played this geographical area had its Triangle titles removed and replaced by "S. A. Lynch Enterprises Presents." Although he no longer owned the stock personally, Lynch retained his position as president of Triangle Distributing by virtue of his control of S. A. Lynch Enterprises and Harry

---

[2] These features were to be released independently of the regular Triangle program and sold to non-contract theaters at a premium price.

Eddie Foy in a rare production still from his only Triangle-Keystone Comedy, A Favorite Fool *(1915). Overly impressed with his stage reputation, Foy's loud and obnoxious presence on the Keystone lot was complicated by his refusal to follow direction and his constant complaining that he was not being treated as a star. Foy and Sennett took an immediate dislike to each other and the other comics placed bets with each other on the outcome of their temperamental clashes.*

Aitken, who had concluded that his problems were nearly over when Triangle Distributing was formed, now found that his bad dreams had suddenly become nightmares of the first order; Lynch was all over the place, asking embarrassing questions and plaguing the promoter for profits—profits which Harry could not have delivered even had he wanted to.

The transfer of Lynch's holdings also brought about an end to a distribution arrangement with Paralta Pictures, which had been negotiated in June 1916. Carl Anderson, Paralta's president, had been convinced by his close friend Lynch that Triangle Distributing was the ultimate outlet for his pictures and accordingly, had agreed to a Triangle contract for distribution, but only as long as Lynch retained an active and personal financial interest in the firm. When Lynch saw fit to bow out financially, Anderson accordingly took the cue and broke his contract.

12

A Rose by Any Other Name

IN THE FALL OF 1917, THE TRIANGLE STORY TOOK A NEW AND interesting twist with the quiet formation of two new companies, the Tower Film Corporation and W. H. Productions. Housed under the same roof at 1457 Broadway, Tower and W. H. Productions were headed by Joseph Simmonds. Designed to cater to the independent market, both organizations were destined to make the reissue of motion pictures a profitable business. Up to then, the industry had regarded the shelf life of its product to be but a mere five years, and vaults were periodically cleared of films no longer held to be of value. Most were callously destroyed, as one would burn the Sunday paper after reading it, with no thought that future generations would be deprived of a means of studying the early cinema's techniques and development first-hand. Although the reissue of a few pictures had previously taken place, the process was usually viewed as a stop-gap measure by industry executives, regardless of how hard their publicity departments had worked to move the merchandise on unsuspecting exhibitors with the slogan "Good Pictures Never Die."

The most successful of the two, W. H. Productions, began an extensive campaign with a small list of retitled Hart features, and predictably, patrons and exhibitors associated W. H. with William S. Hart, parting with their money to see what they presumed to be new Bill Hart westerns. A loud hue and cry soon arose from disgruntled audiences and other independent distributors quickly capitalized on the dissatisfaction by convincing the Federal Trade Commission to move in. Taking time out from his work in Zukor's Artcraft Pictures, Bill Hart issued a series of disclaimers concerning his supposed connection with the firm and then filed suit to stop the re-release of his old pictures under new and different titles.

Initially, W. H. Productions fought tooth and nail for the right to retitle when and as it saw fit, claiming that all product which it released had been extensively re-edited by Hal Reid, with new subtitles and therefore qualified as a "new" picture, but when the FTC threatened to issue a "cease and desist" order, Simmonds retreated to a compromise position, offering to include the old title on the new title card. Patrons who could read (and read fast enough) would then be aware that the film they were about to watch was a reissue. Advertising materials were also to contain the same information and they did, but one marvels at the disproportionate size of the old title and its inconspicuous placement on the one-, two- and three-sheets.

Simmonds worked hard to squeeze every possible cent from the reissues. After the Hart films proved they could earn a profit, W. H. Productions undertook the distribution of hundreds of the Griffith, Ince and Sennett pictures, the majority of which dated back to the product originally distributed by Mutual. At first, prints were sold to exchanges for a flat $80.00 per reel, but after exhausting the exchange market during 1918, certain desirable ones (mostly Chaplin subjects) were then offered directly to exhibitors on an outright sale basis—prints and their ownership were transferred in any desired quantity for $150 a reel.

Many of these films exist today only because of the W. H. Productions reissue. The original Mutual release prints had worn out long before Triangle expired and had the subjects not been re-released, only a slender record of the Ince and Sennett productions of the 1912-15 period would still remain on film.[1] But W. H. Productions literally flooded the market with new prints made from the original negatives which Kessel and Baumann had included in their sale of the New York Motion Picture Company and many have found their way over the years into private collections where they have been preserved.[2]

The success of W. H. Productions, and to a lesser extent the Tower Film Corporation, was most phenomenal and the profit

---

[1] Very few of the total releases were Griffith subjects and as a result, most of the prints which have turned up in recent years have been Ince and Sennett films.

[2] Probably the largest single private collection of the Ince and Sennett subjects belongs to Paul Killiam, who exhibited many of them on his "Movie Museum" television program in the early fifties. Killiam has now made an agreement with Blackhawk Films to release these subjects in 8mm and 16mm for home collectors.

The little dunce is Bobby Vernon; his lovely companion a young Gloria Swanson. Joining Keystone with her husband Wallace Beery from Essanay, Gloria lent her attractive presence to a series of romantic comedies with Vernon. Within two years, Gloria was starring in Cecil B. deMille's sensational "bathtub" pictures and people asked, "Who's Wallace Beery?" Beery came into his own in the late twenties, but Gloria's fame and fortune far outstripped that of the former elephant trainer.

margin huge. Few in the industry would have believed that such a mountain of gold existed in a vault of old negatives, footage which they would have disposed of without compunction. But fewer knew the real story and although many marveled at the prosperity which W. H. had realized from the Triangle vault, while Triangle itself gasped and wheezed to its ultimate collapse, there was a great deal more to the story than met the eye, as we shall soon see.

But the fact that the W. H. reissues were a huge financial success should not come as a great surprise to the reader. As we have already seen, initial Triangle release was limited to the Triangle contract theaters, some 1500 of the estimated 20,000 in operation during 1915-16, or less than 10 percent of the potential market. Most of these were located in the densely populated urban centers, for rural areas could not support the luxury of Triangle's "high-class" entertainment. Even Triangle's own reissue of its subjects reached less than 15 percent of the total exhibition outlets, leaving a huge number of theaters which had never played a single Triangle film. From 1915 on, the total number of theaters in the United States diminished steadily as competition forced the marginal ones out of business and consolidation in the form of chains helped to erode the total, but when W. H. Productions arrived on the scene late in 1917, there were still many thousands of potential outlets which had never been reached, one of the major failings of Triangle's overblown hopes to establish its pictures as the standard. With aggressive marketing by Joseph Simmonds and a reasonable rental scale, the W. H. reissues grossed many times more than the original releases and reached the large audience which might well have saved Triangle from its ignominious fate.

H. O. Davis remained general manager of the Triangle Film Corporation for one year. He found it virtually impossible to get along with Harry Aitken during this time, but despite the interference from his superior, Davis managed to reduce the annual production costs by $2.5 million, returning about $1 million worth of stock (at the deflated value) to the Triangle treasury. Triangle's balance sheet for the fiscal year ending June 30, 1918, showed $49,317 in cash-on-hand and accounts receivable of $68,860. Other assets included a $270,135 interest in other production companies (Reliance, Majestic, New York Motion) and an inventory valued at $130,951. While Triangle still had accounts payable of $189,627 and outstanding loans of $277,630 to retire, by all financial yardsticks, Davis' tenure had been highly successful, especially considering the morass into which he had stepped.

Slim Summerville and Charlie Murray appeared in a large number of the Triangle-Keystone Comedies during 1916–17, usually with Louise Fazenda or Polly Moran in support. Here they quickly hatch up a new scheme in His Precious Life *(1917), one of the last of Sennett's comedies to be released by Triangle.*

To eliminate expensive overlap between production units, Davis had created a new post, hiring Julian Johnson (editor of *Photoplay* magazine) as editor-in-chief for Triangle, giving him complete responsibility for all Triangle pictures from script to screen. An entirely new group of stars had been developed, with Olive Thomas, Alma Reubens, Roy Stewart, William Desmond and Taylor Holmes headlining the casts. The Triangle pictures became program pictures in the best sense of the word, delivering entertainment instead of prestige to those remaining houses which chose to continue exhibiting Triangle Plays. *The Paws of the Bear* was

A Rose by Any Other Name

typical of the new films under the Davis regime. Featuring Clara Williams and William Desmond, the story revolved around the efforts of Miss Williams as a Russian spy to obtain a briefcase containing top-secret documents from an Austrian diplomatic messenger traveling with his American friend. A series of tense situations was strung together in the best melodramatic fashion, as plot and counterplot carried the principals across Europe.

While trade reviewers conceded that it was an interesting film, they criticized it for lacking what they termed "deep sympathetic feeling" (an attribute present in earlier Triangle Plays which had cost them dearly at the box-office) but audiences were more responsive to this subject matter than they had been to *Don Quixote*, *Macbeth* and similar attempts to elevate the taste of the masses. When Mack Sennett left Triangle, the great majority of his player and director contracts remained in Triangle hands and although many left the fold, they gradually returned one by one until the new Keystone and Triangle Comedies produced by Davis again featured a cast of faces familiar to every Keystone fan. While these "bogus" Keystones lacked the precision and polish of the

The home of Keystone Comedies, Sennett's lot had all the aesthetic appeal of a junkyard, but from this congested collection of ramshackle buildings came the best-known screen comedies of any era.

Sennett comedies, many like *Caught with the Goods* (featuring Harry Gribbon) were virtually indistinguishable from the Sennett Keystones produced for Mutual release in 1914-15.

It was clear to any observer that had a man like Davis been placed at the Triangle helm from the very beginning, the firm's future might well have been a good deal more secure, but Harry was very much disgruntled. The Triangle Plays of 1917-18 bore very little resemblance to the concept which had characterized the projected path to fame Triangle was to have taken. In a word, Harry Aitken had seen his dream bastardized, but what hurt even more was the success with which the Davis strategy had worked and, his pride wounded beyond words, Harry could only quarrel with his general manager and complain of quality. Up to a point, Davis was willing and well-qualified to withstand the verbal abuse and long hours of argument. After all, he had survived very well at Universal and any man who could toil successfully in Carl Laemmle's vineyard without having bowed completely to the studio's political system was sufficiently equipped to deal with the insecurity involved in working for Harry Aitken. Besides, Davis had a most favorable contract, compared to his previous position.

Davis had surprised Aitken and many others with his grasp of exactly what made a motion picture studio work. Those under him did not like or understand him and thus chose to regard H. O. as an incompetent clown, but regardless of personality problems and petty jealousies, his performance should only be measured by the financial turnaround which occurred after the departure of Griffith, Ince and Sennett. Although Triangle was not completely back on its feet, the once-dark tunnel into which Harry had led it now had a foreseeable end.

Knowing early in the game that his contract would not be renewed, Davis had taken every opportunity to promote himself by press-agenting Triangle features as H. O. Davis Pictures, mentioning Triangle only in passing and when necessary. This move was not calculated to restore him to good terms with Aitken but Davis was prepared to withstand the static as long as he could get away with it.

Publicly, the departure of H. O. Davis from Triangle was said to result from a disagreement over picture quality; Davis supposedly represented the "big picture—expensive production" viewpoint, while Harry insisted upon "low-budget programmers." Of course, the reverse was the real truth, as anyone who knew the

Triangle product of 1917-18 could discern for himself, but some face-saving explanation had to be given the press; it would not do to admit that Aitken had smarted for nearly a year over Davis and his salary.

Once Davis had departed, Harry personally took over the duties of general manager and cleaned house. Only H. O.'s production manager, Ollie Sellers, was retained and Aitken promoted him to assistant general manager. Sellers was a nice chap who wouldn't exercise any individual initiative without specifically being told to do so, and on this attribute became responsible for executing policies at Culver City which Aitken had decided upon in New York. All but fifteen of Triangle's remaining contract players were released from contract, as Harry's new procedure would be to cast actors on a specific picture basis only. Charles F. Stocking was appointed as head of the scenario department and Dr. Daniel Carson Goodman, who had worked for Aitken before, became his associate editor. In this way, Harry now had a direct pipeline into the story department which would keep him informed of any attempted deviation from policy.

In October 1918, Triangle leased its Culver City facilities to Samuel Goldwyn (Goldfish had legally changed his name) effective November 1 and moved back to the Inceville lot which had been thoughtfully retained by Tom Ince earlier. Three production units and the fifteen remaining contract players made the move and pictures featuring Taylor Holmes, Olive Thomas and Alma Reubens continued to be filmed and released. When he indicated a desire to finish a book he had been working on for some time, Goodman was soon replaced by a *Saturday Evening Post* writer, Nina Wilcox; Harry wanted no authors getting rich on his time.

But Harry Aitken's tenure in this position was to be a short one. On May 9, 1919, Triangle's creditors finally forced the issue and Aitken was moved up to the newly created post of Chairman of the Board. The financial interests of Stephen A. Lynch, Fred Kent and Y. F. Freeman were acquired and the Lynch faction eliminated altogether. The Triangle Distributing Corporation was then brought under the complete control of the Triangle Film Corporation and Percival L. Waters, who had represented the banking interests since March 1918, was elected president and general manager of both organizations.

Waters was an interesting personality in that his absolute blandness made him ideally suited for the job ahead. His working knowledge of the film industry and its internal complications dated back to the old Edison Company and the formation of the Motion Picture Patents Company. His experience with the General Film Company under J. J. Kennedy was sufficient to make him fully cognizant of the ups and downs suffered by a sick organization; after all, he had helped to salvage the maximum value from the collapse of General Film in 1916, retiring from the industry after his work was finished, but his new post at Triangle brought Waters face to face with an equally distressing problem.

Waters began his policy of retrenchment for fiscal stability immediately, negotiating a contract with Sam Goldwyn to sell the Culver City studio for cash. Triangle production activity would also soon cease. Publicly, Waters' task was to rejuvenate the two Triangle organizations, but privately his role was to pay off their debts as completely as possible while gradually liquidating the corporations. This loss of Aitken's position and Percy L. Waters' assumption of control would cost Harry and his reputation dearly.

Harry had put up a bitter fight before the reorganization took place, trying desperately to line up sufficient support to retain his position, but the financial interests had finally reached the end of their patience. Triangle's bills loomed large over his head and every argument he could muster for keeping him in charge could easily be refuted by a page in the corporate books. He had spent nearly four years in direct control of the organization and none of the dreams he had forecast back in the spring of 1915 had come to pass. Triangle Plays had failed at the box-office, the Triangle showcase theater scheme had collapsed, Triangle exchanges did not pay their own way and the corporate image with the nation's exhibitors surely could not have been lower. Aitken had no justifiable position for remaining as Triangle's chief executive; it was that simple.

The end of the Triangle Distributing Corporation as a separate corporate entity came in the spring of 1920. Before Stephen A. Lynch left Triangle in 1919, he had merged his United exchanges with those of Triangle Distributing and in 1920, Percy Waters opened negotiations with Hallmark Pictures Corporation to dispose of the entire operation. Organized in 1919 by Frank G. Hall, Hallmark had set as its goal the establishment of the largest independent production-distribution agency in the business. As Hall was actually anxious to acquire a functioning exchange system to avoid the time and trouble of creating one, to say nothing of the

One of the most versatile actresses ever to work for Tom Ince (the other was Florence Vidor), Bessie Barriscale was a New York girl whose stage career began when she was only five years old. Her career was typical of the anonymity in which most of Ince's actresses labored; later work with Robertson-Cole and Paralta also failed to establish her among the front ranks of screen stars. Bessie played every type of role imaginable, and as a result never established a clear screen personality with which audinces could identify.

cost, Waters saw no good reason why that acquisition shouldn't be the United-Triangle circuit and even went so far as to allow Hall to move his operations into the Triangle Distributing facili-

Except for the Hart features, the Triangle sub-titles were plain and unadorned for the most part; subsequent reissues used the technique explored by Hart's films of placing the text on background art, making the title better fit the scene's mood. Notice that Triangle and Fine Arts used different identification logos.

ties before the completed arrangements were formally and legally consummated.

Frank Hall's profitable (from his viewpoint) dealings with Waters only quickened his appetite for further dealings with Triangle. The idea occurred to him that a considerable sum of money was still left in the oft-squeezed remains of the Triangle vault, and by May 1920 an agreement had been reached. For an undisclosed sum of money, Hall would take over the physical facilities of Triangle Distributing, retaining the exchange personnel and George M. Montgomery as general manager. In addition, he acquired the rights to an extensive list of Hart, Fairbanks and Frank Keenan features, along with sixteen of the Triangle-Keystone Comedies made by Mack Sennett. In addition, he agreed to continue distributing whatever product the Triangle Film Corporation might produce or otherwise prepare for release.

Hall's own grandiose dreams came to a rather abrupt and crushing end three months later when Hallmark went into involuntary bankruptcy. The official reason given for the sudden collapse was a heavy investment in a film featuring boxer Jess Willard, whose loss of a title fight to Jack Dempsey just before its release supposedly ruined the market potential; actually, Hall had made the same mistake so many independents before him had made—he tried to build his empire too rapidly and on a foundation of sand. Listing liabilities of $750,000[3] and assets of $50,000, which included films, fixtures and outstanding accounts, the fledgling empire was placed in the hands of Benjamin DeWitt as receiver on August 14. Hallmark was subdivided into territories and sold off as quickly as possible, with P. E. Meyer of Gorham Photoplays Incorporated taking over the distribution of Triangle films in the large New York-New Jersey area. And so the unprofitable and jinxed Triangle exchange system, which had passed through so many hands and eventually changed its name, had now come to its final inglorious end.

---

[3] The petition for receivership listed the following major creditors: Robertson-Cole, $252,000; Jacob Ruppert, $112,000; Penn Export and Import Company, $177,500 and the British-American Picture Film Corporation, $35,000. The remaining liabilities were scattered among dozens of small creditors. Waters had demanded and received immediate cash for the Triangle exchanges.

13
In the Clutches of a Gang

BUT BEFORE THE TRIANGLE DISTRIBUTING CORPORATION PASSED into history, it proved to be the key which unlocked the door hiding Triangle's real troubles and brought the entire sordid affair to light. Functioning at this point in time under the Triangle Film Corporation, Triangle Distributing negotiated a contract in October 1919 to buy all assets belonging to the K. T. Distributing Corporation. By this time, Felix Kahn, Harry Aitken's long-time friend, financial confidant and member of the board of directors, had partially confirmed old suspicions, and thinking that he recognized a pattern, brought action in the Supreme Court of the State of New York as a Triangle officer, asking for an injunction to restrain the consummation of the contract. It was granted and the contract dropped, but Kahn pressed forward and brought his suspicions to the attention of Percy L. Waters—Harry had finally overstepped himself this time. Acting upon Kahn's information, Waters intensified the task of reconstructing the picture puzzle which Harry's stewardship had made of the company books and slowly arrived at an inescapable conclusion—Triangle's former president and founder had willfully manipulated Triangle for his own ends. The problem of sorting out the various threads and following each to its logical conclusion, gathering sufficient evidence along the way, proved to be a lengthy and quite complicated task, involving over a year's effort.

On January 22, 1921, Percy L. Waters stood before John Preston Phillips, a Westchester county notary public, to sign a summons prepared by Arthur B. Graham, attorney for the Triangle Film Corporation, against Harry and Roy Aitken, Hyman Winnik and Joseph Simmonds. The individual complaints were attested

In the Clutches of a Gang

to by Waters on February 17 and as the story of Triangle's financial affairs unfolded, it became more and more incredible that one man could have so successfully juggled the books for such a long period of time, and in the process misappropriated such fantastic sums of money, as did Harry E. Aitken. The charges levied against him by Percy L. Waters, acting in behalf of Triangle as its chief officer, began by spelling out Harry's relationship to the corporation.

On July 28, 1915, the Aitken brothers had been elected to Triangle's board of directors, which two days later appointed Harry as president. Under Triangle's incorporation charter, the corporate business was to be handled by the board and between its meetings, all power and authority (except for the election of officers and the payment of dividends) was vested in the board's executive committee, composed of Harry and two other directors. As both Roy and Harry Aitken were principal officers and prime managers of Triangle's affairs, and especially Harry, who was president, a large stockholder, a director and a member of the executive committee, Waters charged that both were in a perfect position to exert pressure and influence, legitimate and otherwise, upon the direction in which Triangle moved and he further charged them with dominating the board's every action by virtue of their ownership and control of a large portion of Triangle stock.

How this control came about was also in the complaint made by Waters. Harry was charged with creating a voting trust of 35 percent of all capital stock by combining his interests with those of the Lothbury Syndicate, Incorporated—which he also organized, owned and controlled—and as a result, he served as trustee over this block of stock in addition to ownership and control of that held in his personal name. On July 28, 1915, Triangle had entered into an agreement with the Lothbury Syndicate to acquire 999,500 of its 100,000,000 shares of stock for the sum of $99,950, or .10 on each share, the block of which had a reasonable market value in excess of $1.5 million at the time. As his interests and those of Lothbury were one and the same, it was clearly a case of selling Triangle short at the very outset for personal gain. A few months later, Triangle stock had a market value of $8.75 per share and Harry realized a considerable (but unknown) sum through the sale of certain portions of that held by Lothbury. Aitken also authorized a payment as chief officer of Triangle in 1915 to the Lothbury Syndicate—a sum in excess of $40,000 without consideration. No contract, agreement, understanding or other legal obligation existed to justify the expenditure of such a sum of money in this manner. To outside observers, Triangle's financial picture now took on the appearance of a giant swindle with its very founding.

On February 10, 1916, Triangle had sold all foreign rights to its productions to the Western Import Company, Inc., at a price far below their reasonable market value. Triangle claimed damages in the sum of $1 million and charged that preferential treatment had been given to Western Import when other unnamed companies had made firm offers of a far larger sum. Under the terms of the contract giving Western Import the exclusive foreign distribution rights, Triangle was to be paid a specified percentage on a sliding scale. Western Import never paid back the part of the profits which had supposedly accrued to Triangle by virtue of the contract, nor was any accounting of the books ever made. Western Import was owned, operated and controlled by the Aitken brothers; Roy Aitken was the guiding hand behind its operations in England and on the Continent.

Western Import also figured in several other exotic financial shenanigans. On September 10, 1917, it presented Triangle with a claim for $142,741.65. Harry Aitken authorized payment without question and no proof of such indebtedness could ever be produced on the part of Aitken or Triangle. On September 17, acting in the name of Triangle, Harry had negotiated a contract with Western Import Limited (the British subsidiary) to sell its assets to Triangle for $400,000. Other Triangle board members later claimed that Harry had put one over on them by a clever combination of fraud, misrepresentation and the concealment of pertinent facts. About a year and a half after effecting the transfer of near-worthless assets to Triangle, a value of $500,000 was placed on them and on January 24, 1919, they were sold along with other Triangle assets of substantial value to the Reserve Film Corporation for $250,000. Reserve Film Corporation then transferred the Western Import Limited assets back to Western Import, Inc., without payment of any kind; the Aitkens also happened to own the Reserve operation. In effect, Harry had the personal use of $400,000 of Triangle funds during this procedure, retaining $150,000 outright in addition to regaining his property and during the period it belonged legally to Triangle, he never paid one cent of Western Import Limited's profits into the Triangle coffers, an inestimable loss.

On December 27, 1917, Harry had committed Triangle to a contract with Western Import, Inc., involving the sole exhibition rights to *Mickey,* a feature produced by the Mabel Normand Feature Film Company in 1916, but shelved by Kessel and Baumann as unfit for distribution. When they disposed of the New York Motion Picture Company, the rights to *Mickey* became the property of Triangle. Western Import, Inc., paid $175,000 for a picture which had an estimated fair market value in 1921 of $500,000 and which would eventually gross in excess of $18 million.[1]

Unable to collect payment on the monies owed it by Western Import, Triangle took advantage of the services of one Patrick H. Loftus, who arranged a loan of $95,000 on August 1, 1918, to the New York Motion Picture Company; the sum was later increased in value to a total of $150,000. While the loan was supposedly for the benefit of Triangle, the corporation saw no part of the actual money; it was diverted for use solely by the New York Motion Picture Company, which had by this time fallen into the hands of Harry Aitken, owner of the former Kessel and Baumann property bought with Triangle's money.

While Loftus had acted as agent for the transaction without charge, even Aitken's own company was not free from his financial depredations; Harry authorized the New York Motion Picture Company to turn over $25,000 to him as a bonus for arranging the loan! When the Triangle note came due, it was removed through the good graces of an Ernest Bru until the corporation could pay it in full from current earnings. One year later, Triangle was still so deeply in debt that the outstanding money owed it by Western Import was desperately needed but still could not be collected. This time, a Francis X. Brosnan stepped forward with an offer of $200,000 in cash, which offer Harry accepted in the name of Triangle. He then authorized payment of $50,000 as interest on the loan, but as the money did not belong to Brosnan, the mysterious benefactor did not receive the illegal interest. After all, why should

---

[1] That *Mickey* was a moneymaker could not be denied; this particular feature was the most financially successful film Mabel Normand ever made. A study of the box-office reports submitted to W. H. Productions shows theater after theater grossed phenomenal sums with *Mickey*. For example, the Merrill Theater in Milwaukee took in $5400 on a 15-cent admission during the middle of the influenza epidemic of 1918–19. The Mishler Theater in Altoona, Pennsylvania turned in a three-day report showing gross receipts of $2938.74. These figures were repeated over and over by houses across the country.

1

Norma Talmadge (1) joined Triangle in 1916 with her sister Constance. Norma made charming but insignificant comic dramas for over a year before moving on to become one of the cinema's celebrated actresses in the twenties. As her Triangle films were low-budget, lightweight affairs in which the subtitles carried much of the story, no one film in particular was outstanding in the manner originally promised by Aitken, yet those seen today, like The Social Secretary *(Triangle, 1917)*, remain delightful because of her presence. As the attractive secretary who was forced to assume a disguise in order to get a job (2), she had an opportunity to project an unusual characterization but once Gladden James (her employer's son) discovered the secret, Norma was able to revert to form (3) and after winning over complications caused by the ever-present Mr. Buzzard (played by Erich Von Stroheim) (4), the film came to a happy conclusion. Later to become one of the fabled directors of the twenties, Von Stroheim was just gaining a foothold in the industry with small acting roles at this time.

2

3

4

he? The $200,000 actually belonged to the Aitkens and Hyman Winnik and thus so did the $50,000 interest payment.

In addition to the Reserve Film Corporation, Harry had also organized the Tower Film Corporation and W. H. Productions, Inc. Both of these organizations acquired rights to a large block of Triangle negatives, which included the Keystone, Reliance, Majestic and Ince films of the Mutual period (1912-15), as well as early Triangle productions, for less than $100,000 total payment. The negatives were recut, retitled (in some cases) and reissued on the independent market, as we have seen, grossing an undetermined but fantastic sum, generally agreed upon by those involved as being well in excess of $1 million.[2]

Hyman Winnik's reply to the complaint against him denied knowledge of the alleged acts and claimed that no conspiracy to defraud Triangle existed. He did acknowledge the Western Import contract for *Mickey* and claimed that all rights and properties had been granted him, but that Triangle failed to deliver the complete negative for his use, thereby damaging him to the sum of $250,000, which he now sought to recover in addition to asking that all charges be dismissed.

Joseph Simmonds also denied knowledge of the alleged acts and the existence of a conspiracy in which he supposedly took part. He stated that Tower had contracted with Triangle on February 11, 1919, to obtain reissue rights valued in excess of $50,000 to 156 negatives, for which he paid the sum of $37,500 in advance. Simmonds maintained that only 56 were delivered, but that on October 16, Triangle agreed to turn over the remaining 100, plus an additional eight not originally included in the contract. In return for these, Triangle asked that Tower supply sample prints of certain negatives. According to Simmonds, the requested prints cost him $1,714.84, a sum which Triangle never paid him. His summation asked for damages in the amount of $65,752.46 and dismissal of all charges.

Harry and Roy Aitken admitted only that Western Import Company, Incorporated, was organized under the laws of the State of New York (a fairly safe admission) and that a loan had indeed been made to the New York Motion Picture Company through Triangle in the name of Patrick Loftus and had been renewed through the good graces of Ernest Bru when it fell due. All other allegations were denied and petition made for their swift dismissal. But it was now apparent that Harry Aitken had managed to bilk Triangle out of 3 million dollars at the very least in a little over three years, and that his stock purchase at the outset had cost the corporation an undeterminable but surely a most substantial loss of capital funds. This was pretty good work for any

---

[2] Triangle's complaint estimated the real value of the negatives at a conservative $500,000, claiming damages of $400,000, but it is quite likely that rentals of the W. H. and Tower prints exceeded three million dollars in the two-year period, 1918–19. Independent exchanges across the country went wild over the W. H. Productions releases; the experience of the Gardiner Syndicate in Buffalo was typical. T. R. Gardiner paid the sum of $60,000 for distribution rights to 750 reels in the State of New York. Business was so brisk that only one year later, he had to replace the 750 prints with another set, paying W. H. Productions another $60,000.

1

Produced in cooperation with the U. S. Navy over a half-century ago, A Submarine Pirate (Keystone, 1915) has become one of the classic Triangle-Keystone Comedies, partially because it has been available for viewing in several mutilated versions over the years (while others have not). The half-brother of Charlie Chaplin, Syd Chaplin joined Keystone in November 1914 and quickly gained a reputation as Sennett's most raucous slapstick artist, causing The King of Comedy headaches galore with his routines, which often bordered on being offensive. As the hapless waiter (1) who overheard Glen Cavender and Wesley Ruggles discussing secret plans (2) and decided to commandeer the submarine, Syd purchased the Admiral's uniform which would form his disguise (3). The lady is unidentified (4) but honors for the hilarity belonged to Sid, who gave his best-known performance of an off-again/on-again career which found him managing the more famous Chaplin's business affairs and occasionally performing on his own.

country boy and yet the saddest part of the entire messy affair remained self-evident—both Harry and Roy Aitken would soon be nearly broke.

But for that matter, so would Triangle. Under Waters' stewardship, the corporation had managed to pay off $2 million of the combined indebtedness of the Triangle Film and the Triangle Distributing Corporation between January 1918 and June 1921. In November 1920, Waters had negotiated a contract with The Film

2

3

4

Distributors League, Incorporated, assigning the right to reissue Triangle Plays. Payment in the sum of $877,000 was to be made over a period of 130 weeks and by July 1, 1921, Triangle had received $149,000 on account. As of June 30, 1921, Triangle claimed total assets of $5,375,164.06, in itself a healthy figure, but a study of its financial records shows that of this sum, a whopping $3,845,573.49 was attributed to good will, trademarks and unassigned reissue value of negatives on hand, placing the actual worth closer to $1,500,000, much of which was plant and equipment. But over $680,000 remained on outstanding loans, payment of which was dependent upon collection of the remainder of The Film Distributors League contract. Triangle faded from the scene quietly while its expensive feature films were still grossing more reissue coin than they had ever returned to the corporate vault during their initial release. It is not unfair to say that Harry's grandiose dream and scheme had made many people wealthy, except for those few unfortunate souls who had the misfortune to hold Triangle stock.

Adam Kessel wrote the beginning of the final chapter in October 1923 (some say that it took him that long to recover from the shock after learning the truth of what had happened to Triangle) when he petitioned the courts to place Triangle in receivership for an unpaid claim of $93,930. Judge Learned Hand granted the petition and after placing Percy L. Waters under a $10,000 bond, appointed him as receiver. Waters had not been able to pay off the remaining $680,000 in debts and Triangle went down for the final count. The schedule filed by Waters showed Triangle to have liabilities in the amount of $651,298 and assets listed mainly as being of an unknown value, but which were carried on the corporate books in the sum of $2,260,637.

Finis was thus written to the Triangle Film Corporation and Harry Aitken's dream by Frank W. Severn in January 1924 when he purchased its remaining assets for $55,000 in cash. A 98 percent interest in the New York Motion Picture Company, Reliance and Keystone, ownership of about 1500 negatives and the rights to all Triangle stories constituted the assets. On May 31, 1926, the Commonwealth of Virginia revoked and annulled Triangle's charter for failure to pay its annual registration fee for the years 1924-25. While the dream had taken ill almost with its conception, it took over nine long years to expire.

But if it had accomplished nothing more in its short, unhappy period of activity, Triangle had managed to influence the motion picture industry and the direction in which it would move in the twenties. Harry had opened the door to untapped millions resting in Wall Street, a fact which later producers considered first a blessing and then a curse; the bankers eventually owned most of them. While both First National and United Artists had somewhat checkered careers, they would each apply variations of Harry's concepts in their drive to become dominant organizations in the twenties. Triangle had attempted to elevate the level of literacy in movie entertainment, certainly a laudable gesture even if it was doomed to failure. Triangle's celluloid dramas did not replace the spoken stage, but no other producer again made the same mistake which had almost ruined Zukor at the outset and then entrapped Triangle; Harry learned the hard way that great names do not by themselves make great pictures, with the result that the motion picture sought and reached its own level of quality and content by lessons such as these, becoming a medium of entertainment for the masses.

The salaries paid to stage actors in 1915 had a direct effect upon the industry's wage scale, contributing to the fantastic rise in costs which spiraled on into the twenties. While Harry and

Triangle could not claim direct credit for the consolidation which affected the industry in 1915-17, certainly the threat of Triangle and its potential influenced and even hastened the combination of Zukor and Lasky into the soon-to-be-all-powerful Paramount Pictures, indirectly setting the stage for Sam Goldwyn to cut the umbilical cord and move in his own direction. In doing these things, Triangle could consider itself one of the prime factors which helped to set the stage for the fantastic competition in the twenties when Paramount, M-G-M and Fox raced to gain a monopoly in production, distribution and exhibition. Yes, Triangle had made its impact felt, but what of Harry Aitken?

14

His Busted Trust

HARRY AITKEN'S DISCLAIMER OF WRONGDOING WAS NOT ACCEPTED and the case went to court, with Triangle seeking a judgment that would direct the defendants to:

(1) Cancel all contracts and assignments involved in the specified acts.

(2) Transfer to Triangle all stock, property and rights acquired by or through the contracts and assignments.

(3) Account to Triangle for all profits made through these transactions.

(4) Pay all monies due Triangle as a result of the accounting.

(5) Refrain from disposing in any way of the property or other rights transferred to them by contract with Triangle.

(6) Cease exploitation of any of the pictures involved in the named transactions.

(7) Pay Triangle the court costs and whatever other relief the Court deemed proper to award.

Triangle asked for an award of $2 million plus interest to cover the various named machinations of the individual defendants. When he took the witness stand, a quiet and humble Harry E. Aitken was unable to remember the events of the past six years with sufficient clarity to answer the questions put to him. Even though Triangle's attorney Arthur Butler Graham detailed his activities for him, Harry suffered from an apparent loss of memory. Harry Aitken settled out of court for the sum of $1,375,000 and, holding a briefcase full of near-worthless Triangle stock, sued Stephen A. Lynch for an accounting, a tactic which he hoped would forestall

Sir Herbert Tree in a scene from the artistic Macbeth *(Fine Arts, 1916), the film which taught Harry Aitken the futility of expending large sums of money on production. After this experience, Aitken was only too pleased to see Sir Herbert leave the Triangle roster and no more expensive stars were hired. While* Macbeth *came the closest of the Triangle Plays to living up to Harry's original premise, it was not appreciated by exhibitors or audiences and proved an expensive flop.*

the stock value from further deterioration and give him an opportunity to dispose of it; the tactic failed.

If Stephen A. Lynch appears to be a mysterious figure in the long, involved and sordid history we have just covered, it is as it should be. Lynch was at best an unsavory character, with excellent reasons for maintaining the veil of secrecy that he drew about his activities very carefully. He was no stranger to court proceedings; in 1918 his U. S. Exhibitors' Booking Circuit had been proclaimed an outright fraud by the courts, but Lynch was a large exhibitor whose main wealth came from a more-or-less legitimate source, if you can call his manner of twisting the competition's arms legitimate. There is no record of the manipulations which he carried on at Triangle Distributing during his years of influence but he had not exposed his flanks in the blatant manner of Aitken and thus managed to escape the Triangle debacle with his reputation unscathed and his pocketbook nearly intact. His activities during this period were not publicly noted in the press with the frequency other industry moguls were treated to and he did not seek publicity. As a result, his role in the various conspiracies which swirled about and around Triangle has not and probably never will come completely to light. Strangely enough, without exception, Harry Aitken's Triangle associates, who were perfectly willing to discuss Harry's shortcomings, abruptly denied knowledge of Stephen A. Lynch when his name was brought forth and immediately changed the topic; the impression that his would also be a fascinating story is inescapable.

One great question still remains to be answered and I can give only a partial reply. Why did Harry Aitken set out to revolutionize the motion picture industry and end up in the dishonor and disgrace of having sold out his dream and those who had been foolish enough to believe in it with him, for mere personal gain? Why would a man run the risks that Harry took, gambling his future and reputation on an illegitimate scheme when he had all the tools at hand to make an honest fortune? One could easily envision the likes of Kessel and Baumann draining the life blood from a company, but the well-mannered, well-bred executive image, which Harry projected so very easily, did not lend itself to this sort of corruption—or did it?

Film historians have tended to oversimplify and place the blame for Triangle's failure on the product it turned out in the first year of operation, as mentioned earlier, but this is too easy an answer to accept completely. The truth is, while the Triangle films were bad, they were not that bad. Overlooking their limited distribution for a moment, a look at the Triangle output reveals that Sennett's comedies were responsible for much of the Triangle success, limited as it was, and that Tom Ince's films made money at first; but as Ince tired of the ever-increasing grind, he tended to relax control and in the mid-1916-17 period, the financial performance of his pictures began to slip. It is interesting to note that upon leaving Triangle Ince restricted his output greatly for the remainder of his career, spending much more time with each film and watching his name slip away from the public.

The Triangle Fine Arts productions of D. W. Griffith proved to be the main burden, and for this the blame must be shared by both Griffith and Harry Aitken. Had D. W. concentrated his attention on the day-to-day operation of the studio instead of becoming completely entrapped by his own pride and visions of grandeur, the Fine Arts pictures would probably not have done very much better at the box-office—*The Birth of a Nation* had spoiled "The Master" for the mundane activities of program pictures. Except for his name, Griffith was completely unsuited for the Triangle concept, but even in spite of this and the unpopular pictures turned out by Fine Arts, the Triangle product taken as a whole could have returned a handsome profit to the organization.

Overhead was a distinct and severe problem that could have been brought under control quite easily at the outset. Had Harry not constantly exhorted the producers to spend more money (and bemoaned the fact when they did), Ince and Sennett would have kept a sharp eye on unnecessary costs; at Keystone, the money was literally given away in order to bring negative costs up to the point that the New York office would accept as desirable. Harry seemed to equate great expenditures of money with quality pictures, a correlation that did not necessarily prove to be correct.

The competition provided by Zukor, Lasky and later Goldwyn stood as an important factor, which Aitken failed to properly understand or appreciate. These men were bent on controlling the industry and spent their money wisely. At a time when Aitken was boasting of $100,000 negative costs (but spending only an average $30,000 in reality), Paramount was releasing pictures that actually did cost in the neighborhood of $65,000 to $75,000 to produce, and the bulk of the money was not spent on exorbitant player contracts for unknown quantities, but rather on stars whom the public had created by their own choice. The competition had its finger on the public pulse; Harry was trying to change that pulse to suit himself.

That the stage star experiment was detrimental to Triangle is beyond doubt. Paying Sir Herbert Beerbohm Tree $100,000 to star in a film in which Monte Blue was required to double him, except for the medium and close facial shots, was in effect paying money for the use of a worthless name—the average moviegoer of 1916 had no idea who Sir Herbert was, and probably wouldn't have walked across the street to find out, much less pay his good money to watch a story he couldn't understand.

Thus, overhead, competition, the use of expensive unknowns in stories which the public did not care for, and their very limited distribution were distinct disadvantages, yet in spite of these factors, Triangle was able to exist and earn sufficient profits to allow Harry's diversion of funds in excess of 3 million dollars to maintain his other enterprises. What could it have done without Harry?

But removing these factors from the picture completely still leads one to an inescapable conclusion—had Triangle not been severely undercapitalized at the very beginning,[1] and if Harry's fingers could have been excluded from the corporate purse, Triangle possessed the raw potential for success and could have survived to show a decent profit, although it might not have revolutionized the picture business. And so, regardless of all these other factors, the answer to Triangle's demise still rests with the person of Harry Aitken. Harry died in 1956, but several of his associates are still alive and this question was posed to each. Without exception, all seemed to be in agreement that Aitken was an admirable and respected figure in his own right, but plagued with at least three major liabilities which combined to destroy his perspective.

---

[1] It is a moot question as to whether Triangle was undercapitalized deliberately in an attempt to skim the cream for himself or whether this resulted from Harry's badly overextended assets and a desire to keep Triangle as close to his own business as possible. My own investigation leads me to believe that the latter was the case—the dream began simon-pure and gradually became tainted as time and adverse circumstances forced Harry to compromise himself to the point where he threw caution to the wind and decided to clean house, salvaging all that he could for himself regardless of the ethics involved. By late 1918, it appears that he was the victim of a tremendous inner struggle; while he wanted to liquidate on one hand, covering the overlapping maze of financing, Harry was also torn by the personal desire to resurrect Triangle to the position of glory it had known on September 23, 1915 and continued to tell himself it could be done.

Bessie Barriscale and Bruce McRae in The Green Swamp *(Ince, 1916), a story of jealousy without justification which ruined a marriage and the lives of those involved. Miss Barriscale's deterioration in the role of the loving wife was quite well done.*

His sense of morality involved what has aptly been described as "floating ethics." The game was played by whatever rules Harry chose to follow and the line between his concept of right and wrong was constantly shifting—the end justified the means. Unfortunately

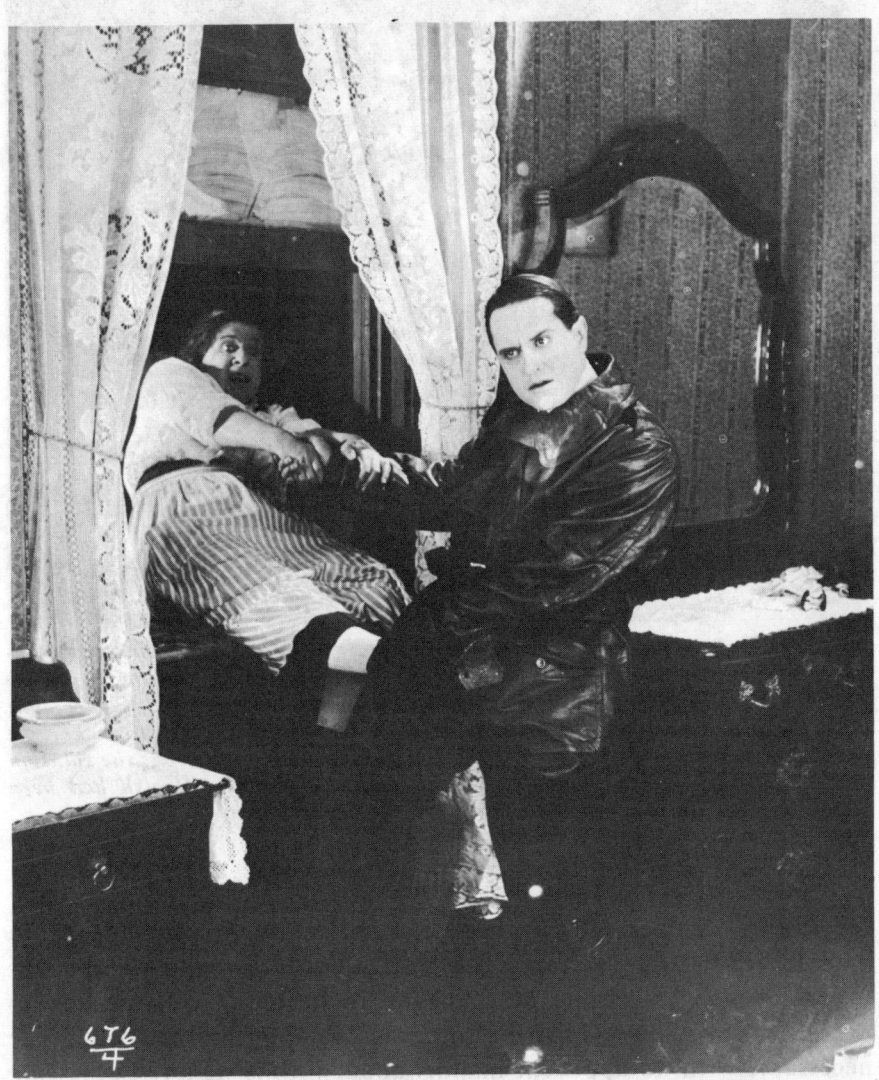

A veteran stage actor, Taylor Holmes came to the movies with Essanay late in 1917, just as the organization was in the process of liquidating its assets. Joining Triangle in 1918, he became one of its few actors to whom audiences responded favorably during 1918–19 and made a number of financially successful light comedies, such as Taxi *(Triangle, 1919). While he never made much of an impact on the silent screen, Taylor Holmes became a much-sought-after character actor in later years.*

De Wolf Hopper played Don Quixote *(Fine Arts, 1916), with an assist from Max Davidson as Sancho and Fay Tincher as Dulcinea. A California rattlesnake was used to represent a Spanish Asp in an important sequence, but once the film was ready for release, it was discovered that rattlesnakes are not native to Spain. As the snake's rattlers were prominently seen, the solution was to carefully paint them out on the negative—George Walsh had been bitten during filming and refused to do the scene again.*

for Harry, he became confused somewhere along the line as to whether the final goal was the welfare of Triangle or that of Harry Aitken and while he managed to keep the two nicely separated in some cases, Harry also tended to blur the lines whenever necessary, with no apparent qualms about inconsistency. Possessing a tremendous capability for rationalization, Harry was able to live with himself quite handsomely.

His second liability was the association with Kessel and Baumann and their New York Motion Picture Company. Although Triangle paid the negative costs upon receipt of the finished negatives at the New York office, and distributed the profits by way of a drawing account to each of its producers, Kessel and Baumann were constantly overdrawn. Putting the touch on Aitken proved to be the only way to keep them going and just when times were pinched the tightest for Harry, Ad Kessel would send Charlie Baumann (both appeared if the amount was very large or circumstances severe enough to warrant a combined plea) with a desperate request for more money to meet their payrolls, etc.

Harry was finally able to shake the two of them from his life in 1916. Baumann flew into the office one Friday late in the year screaming that he had to have $900,000 in cash at once to deposit by Monday. Somewhat bewildered at this erratic behavior on the part of his vice-president, and quite taken back at the sum mentioned, Aitken shrugged his shoulders and drew the line, announcing to Charlie that Triangle simply could not furnish that sum—Wall Street and the banks were both closed. Charlie tried every trick in the book to little avail, but in the process of listening and refusing, Harry discovered a solution to his problem.

Changing tactics, Aitken reassured Baumann that he could probably arrange it after all and picking up the phone, dialed a number. Speaking in a low tone for a moment, he broke into a smile and nodded to Charlie, who slumped back in his chair with a great sigh of relief. After hanging up, Harry told Baumann that they would go to Wall Street together the first thing Monday morning and meet a financial acquaintance who just might see his way clear to putting up the money, if he could be convinced that Kessel and Baumann were worthy of such a large loan. The following Monday, Aitken and Charlie were ushered into a long, magnificent Wall Street office. At the far end of the room was a large ornately carved mahogany desk, behind which was seated a gentleman whose appearance was the model of refined dignity and reeked of wealth.

Baumann quickly explained his need, which the financier readily agreed to help alleviate, but on one condition—Kessel and Baumann were to turn over their Triangle stock and voting rights to him as collateral. Aghast at the proposal, Baumann started to back out, but under Harry's prodding about the desperate situation Charlie had just finished describing, he finally accepted the terms. The stock was delivered and a check for $900,000 placed in Charlie's hands. The New York Motion Picture Company no longer controlled its share of Triangle stock and Kessel and Baumann's single weapon over Aitken's head was removed for good.

When Adam Kessel and Charlie Baumann later discovered that they had been taken to the cleaners by Harry Aitken, their prized patsy, they nearly had a joint heart attack—the entire incident had

Brought to Triangle to do Don Quixote, De Wolf Hopper stayed around to star in several of the Triangle Comedies produced by the Fine Arts studio when Aitken and Sennett had their original falling-out.

been a façade on Harry's part. While talking to Baumann in his office, the weary promoter had dreamed up a stunt and it worked to perfection. The Wall Street office belonged to a friend and Harry had hired an actor to impersonate the financier. Devising the dialogue that would take place between the two men, Aitken had led Baumann like a lamb to the slaughter. The $900,000 was

De Wolf Hopper brought his comic talents to bear on a variety of subjects, ranging from the light-hearted Sunshine Dad *(Fine Arts, 1916)* to a cinematic translation of a favorite baseball poem, Casey at the Bat *(Fine Arts, 1916)*.

Harry's money and the voting rights to the Triangle stock block came into his personal possession. It was shortly after this incident that Kessel and Baumann decided to peddle their New York Motion Picture Company, which Harry then acquired in Triangle's name.

His third liability, and the one which probably contributed the most to Harry's downfall, was his penchant for good living. Along with ego fulfillment, this was without a doubt the strongest motivating factor for Harry's mobile ethical conduct and the unconscious justification for the treatment of Triangle. For once again, his associates agreed that to Harry, Triangle was a real dream from beginning to the end, even though he tried to bankrupt it. Aitken's refusal to accept reality and the wisdom of his three producers when they urged certain reforms was an ego defensive mechanism and had he followed their advice, Triangle could have survived, even with his hand in the till.

How does one reconcile a sincere belief with the urge to destroy that which he has wrought? It could only happen in the movies, which offer Dreams For Sale.

Epilogue

HARRY AND ROY AITKEN WERE FINISHED IN THE MOTION PICTURE business. It was one thing to have your hand in the till, another to get caught doing it, but still a third to lose everything as a result. Variations of what the Aitken brothers had done were a common story in the Hollywood of the post-World War I era; Pat Powers, Hiram Abrams and the Warner Brothers were all involved in unsavory financial affairs; they survived, the Aitkens didn't.

Moving back to Waukesha, Wisconsin, and the family home, they established Tri-Stone Pictures in 1923. From that date until his death in 1956, Harry Aitken lived by exploiting *The Birth of a Nation,* in which he still had an interest via retention of his share in the Epoch Producing Corporation. Harry had taken special pains to exclude that interest from any of his wheeling and dealing, just in case of disaster such as the one which overtook him in 1921.

This was bolstered by dreams of selling the rights to remake the epic story in sound and color. Ironically, a changing social structure made the property worthless; the only part of the original worth the paper it is written on today is the title and with the racist reputation of the story, that is also suspect—no Hollywood producer would or could take a chance on producing the picture as it was written and to make it acceptable today would involve such a radical alteration as to make the new version totally unrelated to the original.

Roy Aitken still lives in Waukesha at the time of this writing and with Al P. Nelson, authored *The Birth of A Nation Story* in 1965, an inexcusable paean to the virtues of his brother, greatly underplaying his own role, which is probably a fair assessment of the part he played in Triangle's affairs. Harry was the hard-driving schemer and promoter, not Roy, who professes bewilderment at

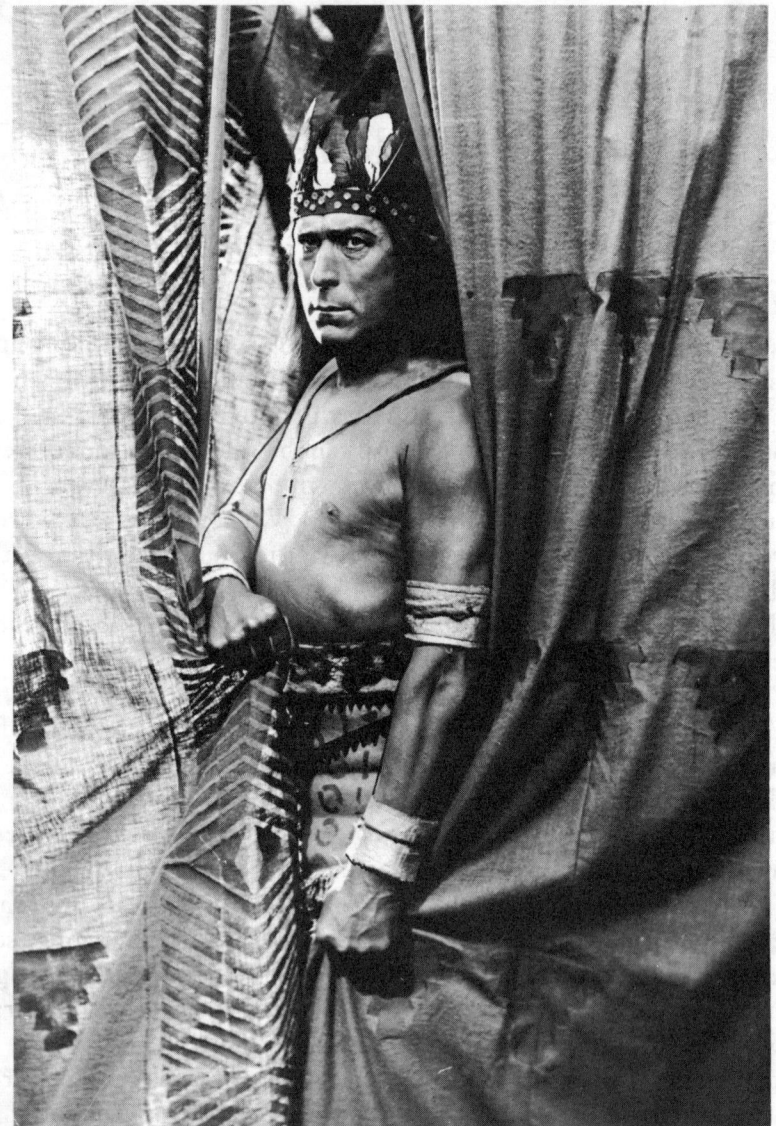

Such offbeat roles as the Aztec chief in The Captive God *(Ince, 1916) gave Bill Hart opportunities for unusual characterizations, but it was his portrayal of the "good-bad man" that had brought him fame. This was produced for $22,678.52.*

some of Harry's activities. Roy continued the operation of Epoch until a few years ago, when Raymond Rohauer (on behalf of Jay Ward) acquired an assignment of the rights which had been willed

Epilogue

by the author of the story from which *The Birth* was made to Mrs. Thomas Dixon, her husband and the third partner in Epoch. Rohauer then forced the younger Aitken out of Epoch by instigating a suit and settling out of court for a reputed $20,000 in exchange for Epoch and its rights to *The Birth*. Triangle was made possible by the fantastic success of *The Birth*; the company expired long ago but the film lives on as a contested artifact of the past. Its supposed ownership by Rohauer and Ward is being questioned at a time when copyright protection is about to expire. The story has now come full circle to its end—or has it?

INDEX

Adventures of Dolly, The, 34
Aitken, Harry E., 15–31, 33, 38–40, 48, 53, 56–58, 69–70, 77–78, 81–82, 84–85, 89–90, 93–94, 98–103, 108–112, 114–15, 132, 134–35, 149–51, 153–57, 161–62, 166, 168–69, 171–73, 177, 180–82, 186–89, 192–94, 196–97–99, 201–204, 206–208, 210–212
Aitken, Roy, 19, 70, 115, 186–88, 193–94, 196–98, 211–12
Ambrose's Cup of Woe, 54–55
American Aristocracy, 44, 140
American Film Manufacturing Company, 21–22
Americano, The, 42
Anderson, Claire, 63
Arbuckle, Roscoe, 52, 76, 131, 138–39
Armstrong, Billy, 117
Aryan, The, 129, 137, 141–42

Balshofer, Fred, 91
Bargain, The, 136–37
Barriscale, Bessie, 82, 86, 142, 183, 203–204
Battle Cry of Peace, The, 67
Baumann, Charles, 16, 22, 25, 39–40, 49, 56, 65, 91–96, 98, 122, 133, 162–63, 206–210
Bennett, Belle, 142
Bennett, Enid, 142
Binns, George, 111
Biograph Company, 20, 23, 34–35
Birth of a Nation, The, 25, 28, 30, 32, 38, 53, 66, 69, 71, 82, 84, 96, 100, 120, 128, 164, 202
Booker, Harry, 62, 132
Burke, Billie, 127
Busch, Mae, 72, 75

Cabanne, William "Christy," 18, 57, 71, 92, 121–22
Carlton Motion Picture Laboratories, 22
Carr, Harry, 119
Casey at the Bat, 209
Caught With the Goods, 180
Cavender, Glen, 139

Chaplin, Sydney, 194–96
Children Pay, The, 121
Civilization, 66–69, 123–26, 145
Clodhopper, The, 140
Collier, Constance, 135
Collier, William, 72–73
Collins, Frederick L., 153–55, 167, 170
Continental Features Corporation, 23
Coward, The, 122, 126–27, 140, 147, 158–60
Cross Currents, 121

Dalton, Dorothy, 61, 163
Daphne and the Pirates, 141
D'Artagnan, 85, 141
Davidson, Max, 206
Davies, Maitland, 119
Davis, H. O., 27, 90, 137–38, 168–69, 177–81
Desmond, William, 75, 80, 82–83, 127, 178–79
Disciple, The, 18, 137, 141
Dividend, The, 147
Dixon, Thomas, 28
Domino Pictures, 111
Don Quixote, 132, 135, 179, 206
Drummer of the Eighth, The, 47
Duell, Holland S., 154
Dunn, Bobby, 114

Edwards, Walter, 140–41
Emerson, John, 41, 71, 116, 134, 140
Enoch Arden, 121
Epoch Producing Corporation, 211, 213

Fairbanks, Douglas, 31, 33, 36–37, 41–44, 50, 57–60, 93, 116, 120, 137–40
Famous Players, 58, 104, 115, 136
Favorite Fool, A, 172
Fazenda, Louise, 62, 110
Female of the Species, 142
Fickle Fatty's Fall, 139
Film Distributors League, Inc., 194–96
Film Supply Company of America, 20
Flame of the Yukon, 142
Flirting with Fate, 42

214

Index

Flying Torpedo, The, 141
Foy, Eddie, 73–74, 172
France, Robert, 158, 167–68
Frazee, Ed, 74
Freuler, John R., 21–25

Gilbert, John, 152
Gish, Dorothy, 93, 120–21, 124–25, 128, 141
Gish, Lillian, 93, 120–21, 125, 130, 141
Glaum, Louise, 142
Goldwyn (Goldfish), Samuel, 108, 112, 114–15, 182, 202
Green Swamp, The, 204
Griffith, D. W., 20, 23, 28, 30–39, 58–60, 66, 69, 71, 77, 100, 106, 116, 118–121, 165, 202
Gypsy Joe, 153

Hall, Frank G., 182, 185
Hallmark Pictures, 182–83, 185
Hamilton, Hale, 132, 170
Hampton, Benjamin B., 102–105, 109
Hansen, Juanita, 117
Harron, Robert, 93, 97, 141
Hart, William S., 17–18, 20–21, 36, 122, 127, 129, 135, 137, 174–75, 212
Hell's Hinges, 21, 24, 129, 137
Henderson, Del, 74
Her Painted Hero, 132, 170
Higby, Wilbur, 87
His Picture in the Papers, 43–44, 140
His Precious Life, 62, 178
Hite, Charles J., 22
Hodkinson, William W., 104, 109, 150–51, 153–58, 167
Hollingsworth, Alfred, 21
Holmes, Taylor, 141, 178, 205
Hopper, De Wolf, 93, 132, 206, 209–209
House Built Upon Sand, A, 137

Idolaters, 142
Imp Pictures, 19, 45, 64
Ince, Thomas H., 18, 22–23, 30, 40, 45–47, 61, 63–69, 77, 85, 115, 122–23, 126–27, 135, 137, 141–42, 144, 166, 170, 202
Innocent Magdalene, An, 130
In the Switch Tower, 47
In the Tennessee Hills, 47
Intolerance, 69–71, 77, 103, 105–106, 116, 118–120, 126
Irish Eyes, 87
Iron Strain, The, 18, 57, 60, 142

Jackson, Joe, 153
Jim Grimsby's Boy, 167
Johnson, Orrin, 86
Judith of Bethulia, 35

Kaelred, Katherine, 147
Kahn, Felix, 27, 186
Kay Bee Pictures, 111
Keenan, Frank, 127, 140, 158–60, 167
Kemble, William H., 164–65
Kenny, May, 93, 112
Kessel, Adam Jr., 16, 22, 25, 39–40, 49, 56, 65, 91–96, 98, 133, 162–63, 196, 206–210
Keystone comics, 131–33, 142, 145–46
Keystone Film Company, 39, 49, 110
Klein, Arthur, 56, 183
K. T. Distributing Company, 186

Laemmle, Carl, 19–20, 49, 63–64
Lamb, The, 18, 37, 57–58
Lasky, Jesse, 104–105, 150, 202
Learnin' of Jim Benton, The, 137–38
Lewis, Ralph, 68
Lieutenant Danny of the U.S.A., 80
Little Liar, The, 97
Little Meena's Romance, 124
Livingston, Crawford, 21, 27
Loos, Anita, 41, 116, 140
Lothbury Syndicate, 187
Love, Bessie, 93, 141, 169
Lucas, Wilfred, 93, 141
Lynch, Stephan A., 155–56, 167–68, 170–73, 182, 199, 201

Mabel and Fatty Adrift, 131–32
Macbeth, 134–35, 179, 200
Mace, Fred, 60
Majestic Pictures, 23, 35, 37, 49, 111
Markey, Enid, 60, 73, 80, 123, 142, 167
Marsh, Mae, 97, 141
Marsh, Marguerite, 67
Martha's Vindication, 68, 141
Matrimaniac, The, 43, 140
Mayor of Filbert, The, 87
McRae, Bruce, 204
Mickey, 189
Missing Link, The, 141
Mitchell, Rhea, 86
Moore, Owen, 19, 64, 93
Mother and the Law, The, 69
Murray, Charles, 62, 132, 178
Mutual Film Corporation, 22–28, 55, 136, 175
My Valet, 18, 60

Naulty, J. R., 50
New York Motion Picture Company, 22, 45, 49, 61, 65, 77, 91–93, 110, 162, 189, 197, 206–207, 210
No-Good Guy, The, 73
Normand, Mabel, 59–60, 75, 131
Not My Sister, 86

Old Folks at Home, 135
Old Heidelburg, 154
On the Night Stage, 136–37
Owen, Seena, 37, 68, 93, 101, 103, 142

Paddy O'Hara, 75
Paralta Pictures, 142, 173
Paramount, 104, 114–15, 150, 198, 202
Pawley, Raymond, 154
Paws of the Bear, The, 178–79
Peggy, 78, 127
Peters, House, 141, 147, 151
Price of Power, The, 67

Raiders, The, 142
Ray, Charles, 127, 140, 147, 158–60
Reggie Mixes In, 41, 140
Reid, Wallace, 128
Reliance Pictures, 23, 111
Rescued From an Eagle's Nest, 34
Reserve Film Corporation, 188, 192
Return of Draw Egan, The, 129
Richardson, Jack, 87
Riesenfeld, Hugo, 78
Rothafel, Samuel L., 78–79
Royal Rogue, A, 117
Rubens, Alma, 142, 178

Self-Made Hero, A, 52
Sennett, Mack, 18, 30–31, 38–40, 60, 71, 76, 107, 110, 129–33, 156–57, 170, 202
Severn, Frank, 197
Sherry, J. Barney, 87
SIG Pictures, 40
Simmonds, Joseph, 174, 177, 186, 193
Smithers and Company, 29–30, 48
Social Secretary, The, 141, 190–92
Sorrows of Love, 82
Spencer, Richard V., 40
Square Deal Man, The, 20
Starke, Pauline, 87
Sterling, Ford, 51
Stewart, Roy, 27, 87, 137–38, 178
Stout, George W., 39–40, 73, 75, 95–96, 133, 143
Submarine Pirate, A, 194–96
Sullivan, C. Gardiner, 60, 66, 124, 136
Summerville, Slim, 62, 114, 132, 178
Sunshine Dad, 209
Stars and Bars, 51
Superpictures, Inc., 150, 153–55, 161
Swain, Mack, 54–55
Swanson, Gloria, 176

Talmadge, Constance, 93, 141
Talmadge, Norma, 93, 141, 190–91
Taxi, 205
Terry, Alice, 86, 142
Thomas, Olive, 113, 142, 178

Tiger Girl, The, 141
Tincher, Fay, 93, 206
Tower Film Corporation, 174, 192
Tree, Sir Herbert Beerbohm, 93, 134–35, 200, 203
Triangle Distributing Corporation, 155–56, 158, 167, 170–73, 181–83, 185–86
Triangle Film Corporation:
 Bankruptcy, 186–90, 191–94, 196, 199
 Directors, 71
 Exchange system, 50–53, 150, 154
 Exhibitors, 88–89, 164–66
 Exploitation, 88
 Financing, 28–30
 Formation, 48
 Income, 77, 177, 196
 Incorporation, 48–49
 Merger talks, 102, 108–115
 Opening night, 15–16, 18–19, 60
 Player roster, 56, 108, 141–42
 Production, 49, 132, 156, 165–66, 168, 181
 Production costs, 82, 84–85, 88, 127, 129, 133, 147, 161, 202–203
 Production facilities, 56, 61, 77
 Reissues, 174–75
 Reorganization, 182
 Reviews, 57
 Salaries, 72–73, 82–83
 Stage stars, 56, 71–74, 83–84, 134–35
 Stock, 89–90, 149, 187
 Theatres, 50, 53, 78–81, 149
Turpin, Ben, 143

Ulman, Ethel, 68, 147

Vernon, Bobby, 176
Villa of the Movies, 114
Vitagraph, 109

Ware, Helen, 121
Waters, Percival L., 181, 183, 186–87, 197
Weber and Fields, 74, 118, 142, 145–46
Western Import, 188, 189, 193
Western Import, Ltd., 188
Westover, Winifred, 26
Wharf Rat, The, 97
Whither Thou Goest, 86
W. H. Productions, 17, 136, 174–75, 177, 192
Wife and Auto Trouble, 72
Williams, Clara, 147, 179
Winged Idol, The, 147
Winnik, Hyman, 186, 192–193
Wolf Woman, The, 142
Woods, Frank, 58, 148
Worst of Friends, The, 118

Zukor, Adolph, 15, 35, 85, 104–105, 108–109, 112, 114–15, 150–51, 153–56, 202

MINNEAPOLIS PUBLIC LIBRARY

Please leave the transaction and book cards in this pocket.

The borrower is responsible for all materials drawn on his card and for fines on overdue items. Marking and mutilation of books are prohibited, and are punishable by law.

1973